The Autobiography of Sir Götz von Berlichingen:
A Knight of the Holy Roman Empire

The Autobiography of
Sir Götz von Berlichingen

———◆———

A Knight of the Holy Roman Empire

Translated by

JULIUS MORITZ

ANTELOPE HILL PUBLISHING

Translation Copyright © 2022 Antelope Hill Publishing

First printing 2022.

Original manuscript *(Rossacher Handschrift)* from 1567 was edited and published as *Ritterliche Thaten Götz von Berlichingen's mit der eisernen Hand* by Verlag: Pforzheim Finck, 1843, and translated from German by Julius Moritz, 2021.

Cover art by Swifty.
Edited by Rollo of Gaunt.
Interior formatting by Margaret Bauer.

Antelope Hill Publishing
www.antelopehillpublishing.com

Paperback ISBN-13: 978-1-953730-25-1
EPUB ISBN-13: 978-1-953730-26-8

CONTENTS

────◆────

Editor's Foreword vii
Translator's Note xi
Introduction 1

CHAPTER ONE
Part I 3
Part II 12
Part III 16
Part IV 24
Part V 27
Part VI 28
Part VII 39
Part VIII 40
Part IX 46
Part X 51
Part XI 64

CHAPTER TWO: THE PEASANT WAR
Part I 81
Part II 90
Part III 93
Part IV 95

CHAPTER THREE:
SOME RIDING STORIES OUTSIDE OF THE FEUDS
Part I 97
Part II 100
Part III 102
Part IV 103
Part V 105
Part VI 107

v

Gottfried "Götz" von Berlichingen was born in 1480 in Jagsthausen, in the South German region of Swabia, in the Holy Roman Empire. He died on July 23rd, 1562, in his castle in Hornberg. He was buried in the Schöntal Monastery. He was married twice, first with Dorothea von Sachsenheim and from 1517 onwards with Dorothea Gailing von Illesheim. He had three daughters and seven sons, five of which died in their early childhood.

EDITOR'S FOREWORD

◆

Gottfried "Götz" von Berlichingen (1480–1562) is not quite a household name, but still one that has left its mark on history. The famous (or infamous, depending on who you ask) knight was first enshrined as a German folk hero by Johann Wolfgang von Goethe's eponymous 1773 drama. He belonged to a class of smallholding Imperial Knights from Swabia in South Germany, a notoriously fragmented and rambunctious region in those days. Swabia in the old days of the Holy Roman Empire had been a center of Imperial power, and a rival of the other powerful "stem duchies" of Franconia and Saxony. The powerful Hohenstaufen family ruled it for a time, and also ruled as Holy Roman Emperors, Kings of Sicily, and (at least nominally) as Kings of Jerusalem. The downfall of the Hohenstaufen dynasty produced chaos throughout the Empire, but especially in Swabia.

Near-constant political intrigue and petty warfare, combined with the region's close involvement in Imperial affairs, allowed Götz along with many of his peers to achieve high renown within the Empire. Some of these peers included the father of the Imperial Landsknechts, Georg von Frundsberg, and the rebellious knight Florian Geyer von Giebelstadt. All three would later give their names to Divisions of the Waffen-SS during the Second World War (respectively, the 8th *Florian Geyer*, 10th *Frundsberg*, and 17th *Götz von Berlichingen*), underlining their high status in German folk history.

The story of Götz von Berlichingen's life is a fascinating one, and his first-person retelling of his adventures includes many humorous elements alongside the more serious and matter-of-fact. This edition has been translated from the original text of Götz' manuscript, the *Rossacher Handschrift*, written in the rough dialect of his native Swabia. As is the norm with our translations, readability has been prioritized, but some of the roughness of Götz' dialect has been left as-is to faithfully convey the character of the original. Some of the translations are imperfect or took a certain amount of guesswork, which the kind reader must forgive due to the wildly divergent spellings and abbreviations used in the original.

Footnotes have been added liberally to clarify idioms, geography, dates, and other terminology that Götz, writing for a contemporary German audience, took for granted. Some of this terminology, especially the political nomenclature, may be confusing to a reader unschooled in the intricacies of the German (Holy Roman) Imperial system of feudal government. Authority was often tied up in a complicated web of familial ties, regional networks, oaths, contracts, alliances, personal feuds, Church authority, and intermediate hierarchies, all interacting with each other. Arguably the most important element of rank was Imperial Immediacy, a term that describes a landholding noble lord subject only to the emperor himself, and who at times enjoyed quasi-sovereign status. Such nobles are often referred to as Princes or *Fürsten* regardless of their actual rank, and had certain rights not held by nobles who were subject to other liege-lords. The most powerful among these were the *Kurfürsten*, or Electors, seven in total, who held the privilege of electing the next heir to the Imperial throne. As this book is intended to be a story of Götz' life and not a history textbook, however, I have tried to give explanations that are as detailed as possible without inordinately expanding the already sizeable number of notes.

I have also maintained German titles in most places (Kaiser for Emperor, Herzog for Duke, Graf for Count, etc.) while providing translations and explanations in the notes. English place names are used where appropriate (Saxony, Bavaria, etc.), with German place names where no English equivalent is in common use. I have further maintained the German "von" when part of a name, but use the English "of" when referencing a ruler's title (Götz *von* Berlichingen, Herzog Friedrich *of* Saxony). These choices are stylistic in nature and may not be perfectly consistent in all cases.

One might wonder why this particular book has been selected for an English translation at the cost of countless hours of labor. Götz offers us no particular political ideology, certainly not any which would be especially relevant today. In many ways he is not a particularly moral man either: even in his own words he often appears vain, willing to bend the truth to suit his own image, prone to petty violence over minor slights, and quick to commit robbery and ransom for no particularly good cause. One would have good cause to question the veracity of many of his statements.

My answer to this is a simple one: Götz is not a paragon, but he is a great man. He is fiercely loyal to his friends and kinsmen, giving his service freely and always being the first to volunteer, gracious in accepting the aid they give to him in return. His attitude towards death and danger is cavalier, leading him to dare where other men would not. He earns respect even from his enemies, while those who fail to respect him often learn the hard way. He lived for eighty-two long years, itself no small feat, and fought as a mercenary knight well into his later years. Even the loss of his arm could not stop him. Instead of retiring or drowning himself in misery, he had an iron prosthetic fitted to the stump of his right hand and carried on his feuding, earning the nickname "Iron Hand Götz" (and providing the inspiration for the character Guts, the Black Swordsman, from the series *Berserk*). His famous quip, "he can lick my ass," immortalized by Goethe and Mozart, sums up his blasé pugnacity rather well. It is only much later in his life, as an old and probably quite exhausted man, that he has any cause for regrets or shame.

Götz von Berlichingen was, simply, a man filled with an abounding love of life, an unquenchable desire to throw himself into the world without reservation. He was not restrained by an overbearing civility or even by the law, but wanted above all to win fame, honor, and respect from those around him, and do right by those who had done right by him. He was truly one of the last knights of romance. In a time where most souls are shriveled and dusty from disuse, such a figure shines all the brighter.

There are, of course, other reasons as well. The history itself is often fascinating, especially for those who come to this book with a preexisting interest in Germany, Feudalism, or the era of the early Protestant Reformation. Those in our audience who have only a cursory knowledge of the era may find it interesting to get an inside perspective on an era that is usually only depicted in sweeping generalizations. It is also simply an enjoyable read, which is only enhanced (in my opinion, anyways) by the sheer historical curiosity of reading something written in the Holy Roman Empire of the sixteenth century.

Lastly, I would like to express my heartfelt thanks to the translator for bringing this wonderful work to us. It has been a pleasure to edit and compile this translation. To the reader, whatever your reasons for opening this book, I sincerely hope that it brings you joy and courage in facing all the hardships and wonders of life.

Rollo of Gaunt
Editor

TRANSLATOR'S NOTE

——◆——

The situation of the Holy Roman Empire at the end of the medieval era is for the average person, even in Germany, a very complicated and largely unknown topic. Even among audiences interested in history, it is often explained dismissively as a decentralized and confused political mess. While this assessment may be true in some ways, the truth is far from incomprehensible. However, this situation, even among the Empire's contemporaries, was undeniably unique.

The available literature that does exist focuses on state policy and territorial changes, rather than the relationship of individuals and smaller groups to the political apparatus, losing the human element necessary to understand the function of historical political organs. The actions of Emperors like Maximilian I and Charles V, whose wars are well known, are usually the exception. The stories of knights like Götz, who actually lived in the Empire and dealt with its unique qualities on a daily basis. is almost unknown, especially in the international world. Hopefully, this translation will change that.

Götz von Berlichingen is a perfect example to represent the struggle of late German knighthood. The lower nobility in late medieval times was a shell of its former self. It had been impoverished by declining populations, rising labor costs, and radical increases in the costs of financing their lifestyle and duties. The lower nobles were also losing their old bureaucratic positions to the newly developing urban middle class. At the same time, they were faced with political struggles inside of the Empire stemming from the Reformation, forcing many of them to fight just to hold on to what they had left. Götz' autobiography shows many aspects of the unique situation of Germany at the time, both good and bad.

As the translator, my goal was to keep Götz' unique personality alive in the English translation as much as possible. I ask nothing more from the reader than to see Götz as a real man of his time, just as we can only be men and women of our own less troublesome period. He was a man who was faced with difficult choices to secure his country, region, and family, and if one truly wants to make a judgment of him, they should do so with this in mind.

This translation is written from no other desire than to share the history of Götz, Swabia, Bavaria, and Germany as a whole with the world.

Julius Moritz
Translator

INTRODUCTION

◆

Salutations,
 To the honorable Hans Hoffman, Mayor of Heilbronn, and the gentleman Stephan Feierabend, the good Licentiate and Syndic[1] himself.
 Götz von Berlichingen, of the Iron Hand.

My especially dear sirs, my good patrons and friends! Even before you, many men and good friends have asked of me for many years, for the honor of my heirs, children, and descendants, to tell everything I have done my whole life as a young noble knight and as a simple cavalryman, in Fehde[2] and

---

[1] A Licentiate is a recipient of a Medieval postgraduate degree, higher than a Baccalaureate but inferior to a Master's or a Doctorate. It gave the holder the privilege to teach in Medieval universities. A Syndic is a type of magistrate or institutional representative, holding various types and degrees of power depending on the context.

[2] Fehde (eng. *Feuding*) was an ancient Germanic tradition wherein the nobility acted out justice between one another without consulting a neutral third party or a court. Because of the non-governmental nature of medieval society, bringing a case before court was often difficult and states often did not even have the power to enforce the courts' decisions anyway. Nevertheless, Fehde had certain customary restrains, such as the requirement that one's opponents be notified before beginning a feud. Fehde is therefore also called the "Anarchy of the Nobility." This changed strongly during Götz's time and Fehde was made illegal in 1495. The practice could not fully be stopped until the late sixteenth century for multiple reasons, including opposition by the nobility, lack of

1

in service for the dear Imperial-Roman majesty, at the call of Kurfürsten[3] and others, both of my own volition and at the request of friends, in troubles both my own and those of others.

To fulfill this request, I now want to put to pen the wars and feuds, which I have participated in for ages, against both higher and lower nobility. Therefore, I have thought and concluded, (if the dear Lord gives me His grace), for the honors and enjoyment for my heirs, descendants and friends who have such interest in my deeds, to collect and write these onto paper.

Therefore, this is what I did during these times, as best as I can recall from my memory. I do this not to seek fame or for lofty titles, but solely for personal reasons: Because resentful folk could mischaracterize my actions out of jealousy and hatred, or maybe because they do not know any better.

To these people, I want to respond by portraying the true reality of what happened from my childhood onwards and nothing else. I expect that nobody shall take exception to this deed, and I hope that everyone understands and accepts it. For this privilege, I want to genuinely thank everyone.

Imperial interest in enforcing the ban, and the lack of resources within the HRE to effectively crack down on offenders. The history of legal feuds should be fairly well-known to the English reader, as it persisted throughout England and the rest of Western Europe during the same period.

[3] Electors of the Holy Roman Empire.

CHAPTER ONE

◆

PART I

The first part concerns my parents, and also my elder siblings; also, my old squires and maidens who were at my service. I often heard that I was a marvelous young child. Everyone noticed from my behavior that I was meant to be a man of war and horsemanship. How people came to this conclusion I cannot recall. What I do know, is that my mother often requested for me to visit strangers, so I could study and learn. As my mother requested, so it would be, and I was often asked to help out relatives, as it will presently be told.

At first, I entered school for a year. I lived with my cousin whose name was Kunz von Neustein, and who lived at Niedernhall, where he built himself a residence. But when I did not show much interest for school, but instead for horses and riding, and was often seen acting upon these interests, my cousin Sir Konrad von Berlichingen took me in and I became his squire for three years. The first journey I accompanied my cousin on was to Markgraf[4] Friedrich of Ansbach in the year of

---

[4] Eng. "Margrave," a high-ranking Count, historically those in charge of a military borderland, usually in Eastern Germany, but by Götz' time a hereditary title conferring rank in the same class as that of a Duke. Götz typically uses the title alone to refer specifically to the Margrave of Ansbach.

1495 for the Wormser Reichstag[5] as a princely consultant. With him I had to travel to the Reichstag, and became a Reisiger[6] from that point onwards. During the first fasting week[7] we arrived in Worms. The first journey began in Ansbach and went to Schrozber, where my cousin's castle was, then further to Moßbach and to Heidelberg. We stopped for breakfast at Hirsch, and after this bite we rode all the way to Worms on the same day.

Therefore, we rode around eight to nine miles a day. This was very tough for my young squire self. But since this time, I have become used to it and traveled many long journeys in very few days and nights, eating and drinking little while doing so.

My cousin was one of the first arrivals at the Reichstag in Worms. He remained there until all the Kurfürsten and lords of higher and lower standing, either in person or through their diplomats, were present at the Reich council. Of those three years I spent with my cousin, Konrad von Berlichingen, many were spent in Worms, Ulm, Augsburg, and other places where lords, Kurfürsten, and even the Kaiser[8] himself, besides on the great Reichstage,[9] came together. So much was demanded of my cousin in these undertakings that he could never spend more than two months in his castles, of which he had three, and even when he arrived, there were so many troubles among the Franconian knights and his good friends that even as an old knight he could never enjoy much peace. And I was beholden to ride along with him as a squire and aid him through his duties.

The last Reichstag I spent with my cousin was the one at

---

[5] The Imperial legislature often met in the city of Worms, including for the infamous 1521 Diet of Worms to which Martin Luther was summoned.
[6] Mounted soldiers or armed guards for journeys and convoys, lit. "Traveler."
[7] The first week of Lent, beginning forty days before Easter. In 1495, this would have been the last week of February.
[8] The Holy Roman Emperor
[9] *Reichstage* or Imperial Councils were formal assemblies of the German nobility; Götz notes that important individuals sometimes met informally in these cities as well.

Lindau on the Bodensee. We arrived by St. Lawrence's Day,[10] and he died the same evening. His knights, and myself as his squire, took his body to the Monastery in Schöntal. Even Berthold von Henneberg, the Bishop of Mainz, showed his dearest condolences and walked in procession with us from the Lindauer Gate to beyond the long bridge which leads across the Bodensee. It was this Bishop of Mainz who was the Erzkanzler[11] of the Kaiser. No Fürsten[12] showed up in person, but every level of the Empire sent their consulates and advisors in their stead. We took the body and went on our way to Heilbronn[13] to spend the night in an Inn called the "Spiegel."[14] That night a large fire broke out in Heilbronn, such that after we ate dinner, we had to stay in the Inn and weren't able to go out. At first light we moved on to Schöntal, where my cousin was finally buried.

Soon after Pentecost[15] I visited Markgraf Friedrich, who gave his dearest condolences. His ostiary[16] was Hans Berlin von Heilbronn, who became my and the other squires' teacher. Right after this, the campaign in Upper Burgundy[17] began. In this war Sir Veit von Lentersheim led some knights, and there I got the permission of my dearest lord and master to accompany the Master of Lentersheim. There was an important Reichstag in Freiburg in Breisgau at the same time,

---

[10] August 10th

[11] The Arch-Chancellor, highest dignitary in the Empire. The position was perennially held by the Archbishop of Mainz and was responsible for overseeing much of the official business of the Empire, especially the Imperial elections.

[12] A Prince of the HRE, referring specifically to a ruler directly subordinate to the Emperor and having no other liege-lord.

[13] A city in northern Swabia, north of Stuttgart.

[14] Eng. "Mirror."

[15] The seventh Sunday after Easter, usually in late May or early June.

[16] Title meaning an armed gate/door guard, here probably a more ceremonial title.

[17] The area between the Upper Rhone river and the Swiss Alps, today mostly corresponding to the Bourgogne-Franche-Comté (Burgundian Free County) Region of France.

where we had to stay for a fortnight. When all of our Haufen[18] by foot and horseback arrived in Ensheim in Upper Alsace[19] and were supplied and ready, we started marching into Burgundy. We occupied a few places and were wearing our armor day and night and on the march. When we arrived before Langres at the evening of St. Jacob's Day[20] we made camp. Multiple knights and three Burgundian cuirassiers who were under the command of my master were brought down by the great heat of that day. They fell off their horses as if they were drunk, even though they did not see any wine that day. Right when we were about to head out in the morning of St. Jacob's Day, a great storm arose that flung hail as big as chicken eggs, such that a Landsknecht[21] who tried to crossed the street was struck onto the ground by them. Therefore, we had to remain where we were until the weather changed. After we marched several miles of the route, we could still see these hailstones on the ground now and then, even though this was during such a suffocating heat that, like earlier mentioned, many knights were brought down by it. After having marched day and night, we arrived near Langres. We dearly wanted a brawl with the enemy, but this did not happen. In a forest we waited through the night until daytime. Our captains said that when the enemies come out of Langres we would cut them off from the city. But the enemy did not show themselves, because they, as the saying goes, "smelled the roast."[22] We then marched past Langres over a big field, the city and the castle to our left, with and the enemies observing us from the city and castle. Therefore, our captains positioned us in a long line and put

---

[18] A medium-to-small military unit, literally meaning "heap," "pile," or "mob." Usually connected to the famous formations of the Swiss Pikemen and the Landsknechte during the sixteenth century.
[19] The Imperial lands on the left bank of the Upper Rhine.
[20] July 15th
[21] Professional German infantrymen often employed by Kaiser Maximilian, founded by Sir Georg von Frundsberg.
[22] South German saying meaning to sense a trap.

much space between us so that our Haufen looked bigger, because we were weak and had not much more than seven hundred horses and two thousand Landsknechte. Even though many more Haufen were with us earlier, they were not with us at Langres. We now made camp in a village not far from Langres, when we got seriously startled and had to get back in position. My master had a squire or baggage boy who was thirty years old and accompanied Master Veit von Lentersheim on three marches, but he acted so clumsy and slow with the horses that he had not fully equipped one by the time I had saddled all the rest of them. Therefore, I gave my master his armor, helmet, and lance, and remained with him while we cleared camp.

We marched until late night and arrived at a different village, which even had a small castle and a bathhouse. Sadly, it was a French village, and therefore the food had all been taken. Food for the horses was plenty and the staples were supplied, but God thankfully gave us chicken and eggs in this emergency, which we cooked up in the morning and which filled us with joy. We had just prepared the food when an order came in to march out and burn the village. We then had to put the bridles on the horses and load our equipment on their backs, but the village was already rising up in flames to such a degree the horses started jumping like goats. We therefore had to break camp and move on quickly, so neither we nor the horses had much food for another three days and two nights.

Next we rode on towards Thann, which is in Sundgau,[23] where we rested for a while until we were ready again. We then marched through Lothringia[24] where Kaiser Maximilian joined us with many hundreds of knights. Among these were the Brothers Herzog Friedrich and Herzog Hans of Saxony, who arrived with the Kaiser from Freiburg and who had as their destination the cities of Toul and Metz. We therefore quickly

---

[23] A Habsburg territory to the south of Alsace on the Lower Rhine, on the Swiss border.
[24] The region northwest of Alsace, called in French "Lorraine."

marched on, because Master Ruprecht von Arenberg was nearby with his warriors. Kaiser Maximilian attempted to beat him there, so as to have the advantage and defeat him, so we had to march with great haste. We ended up arriving too late and Ruprecht was one day ahead of us. We then continued to march to Metz, where we remained for a fortnight, then marched to Brabant,[25] where we rested for only a short time, and then from there to Namur.[26] Winter then began and my master organized the manufacturing of winter clothing, so that we had to remain there for a couple of days again. Around St. Martin's Day[27] or even later, we arrived in Ansbach again. This war was one year before the Swiss Wars.

As soon as we arrived at home, I asked my master for permission for holiday in Jagsthausen,[28] because my father passed away that summer and I intended to take care of my mother and siblings. I stayed until Shrovetide[29] with my family in Jagsthausen. After this I was trained by Markgraf Friedrich as his honor-squire in waiting, at his great table with many other squires. One evening, I had to sit next to a Polechian[30] who groomed his hair with eggs. Luckily, I was wearing a long harness, which Veit von Lentersheim had made for me in Namur. When I then got up next to the previously mentioned Polechian, my harness brushed his pretty hair. He then jumped up from his chair and stabbed at me with his butter knife, but missed. This angered me, but I still picked my short rapier instead of my long one and punched him over the head with it. I still went on to do my tasks of the day, as was tradition, and remained the night inside the castle. In the early

---

[25] A former Imperial duchy, today in central Belgium, around the city of Brussels.
[26] A city south of Brabant, at this time located in the County of Flanders.
[27] November 11th
[28] Götz' home town, located in the modern German state of Baden-Wurttemberg.
[29] The season directly preceding Lent.
[30] An archaic Medieval term for the Poles.

morning the Markgraf, a God-fearing man, went to church, and when we were leaving the church and went back to the castle, the gate was shut down behind me and the marshal came down to me and told me to surrender. I responded therefore with the unfriendly words: "Inconceivable, leave me untouched. I have to go up to the young princes." The good man was smarter than me and let me go. If he had attacked me, I surely would have defended myself and would have gotten myself into even greater misery. I therefore went to the princes and told him what happened between me, the Polechian, and the marshal. They were about to go breakfast and said I should remain where I was, and if someone came into the chambers, to hide in the back room and lock the doors from the inside. I locked myself inside until the princes returned. They reported of their attempt to speak to their father and their dearest royal mother about me but it was of no success. They asked the king to forgo my punishment, but this wasn't possible. The old Markgraf insisted that I had to be thrown into the tower if he wanted a good wife, and the princes, a gracious mother. The princes told me to not resist, for they shall only jail me in the tower for a quarter of an hour. I still responded: "For what shall I be in the tower at all; it was the Polech who attacked me first!" They sincerely promised, though, that I should not remain in the tower for longer than fifteen minutes. I let myself be convinced and willingly went into the tower. Prince Georg wanted to give me a velvet coat decorated with martin and sable fur so I could cover myself, but I asked, "What I should do with this? It's all the same to be in the shit or next to it. If the punishment is so short, it doesn't matter anyways." The princes remained loyal to their promises and gave me up me after the agreed upon time, when my brave captain arrived, Sir Paul von Absberg, who then released me. I had to explain to him the situation, and this brave knight then took me before the court. He vouched for me and apologized on my behalf. All the squires and senior squires, around fifty or sixty, stood around me, and Paul von Absberg passionately spoke that the Polech should also be arrested, but he did not succeed at this.

After around a quarter of a year, another Polech and the Master of Wolmershausen planned a tournament against each other. The man from Wolmershausen was a close friend of Zeissolf von Rosenberg, who got into such a feud with the Polech that they argued it out with their weapons. I stood close by and jumped in when Zeissolf couldn't get close enough to the Polech with his weapon, and the Polech was preparing to thrust his pike at him. Standing right between the pike-haft and the Polechian, I shouted: "If you follow through, I shall beat you on the head so hard you shall catch the plague!" He held his thrust, and the pike clanged off Zeissolf's armor. I then stepped back and acted with restraint, because of my previous troubles with the other Polechian. The very same Polech who I previously beat on the head in the court then came alone and wanted to avenge himself. The opportunity was good, because I was also alone, neither of us having any companions with us. I did not wait long, but jumped towards him and put him to flight. He made his escape to the residence of the Herzog of Lithuania[31], whose servant he was. I would have done far worse to him if he did not thus escape. It became such a big turmoil that nearly one hundred people spectated us from the market or from their windows.

It occurred around this time that Landgraf[32] Wilhelm of Hesse, the father of the current Landgraf,[33] married his first wife. The marriage took place in Kassel. During this event I was made squire of my master Markgraf Friedrich's son Georg.

Once around this time I visited one of my dear friends

---

[31] Duke (*Herzog*) Alexander I Jagiellon of Lithuania. Lithuania at the time existed in a union with Poland, but Duke Alexander split the thrones with his brother, and would not become King of Poland until 1501.

[32] Eng. "Landgrave," another title for a high-ranking Count, similar in status to the aforementioned "*Markgraf*" but without any specific political origin or responsibilities. Götz typically uses the title alone to refer specifically to the Landgrave of Hesse.

[33] Likely referring to Wilhelm III of Hesse and his son, Philip I "The Magnanimous," who succeeded his father in 1504.

named Joachim von Arm. When we both wanted to go to the court, my friend got into an argument with a trumpeter in front of his residence before we could even get into the castle. I saw them both go for their weapons. It occurred to me that this trumpeter had recently struck a Seckendorfer nobleman on the head so badly that nobody expected the nobleman to survive. So, when the trumpeter grabbed his weapon, I ran up to him and grabbed him. We tumbled to the ground, where I managed to take his weapon, but I was injured during the brawl. I do not know if the trumpeter or my own friend hit me. The wound across my head was around one finger long, enraging me to the point that I threw myself at the trumpeter once again. He slipped through my grasp and escaped into his residence. It was fully dark at this time of evening and I did not know anybody else in that residence, or else he would have not gotten away this easily. The wound worried me because we wanted to march on in eight or ten days after the marriage, and I didn't know if it would prevent me from wearing my iron helmet. In the end I was able to adjust it so that I would still be able to march.

Part II

As written before, I spent the days of winter until Lent with my mother and siblings, during which time the war with the Swiss began.[34] The Markgraf had already sent out two armies, when I thought to myself: "Why should I stay here?" I was already bored in Jagsthausen. I therefore rode to Ansbach to hear about what had happened. When I arrived at the court the dear master, Markgraf Friedrich, called his servants and told them to send for the tailor. The tailor arrived and the Markgraf spoke to him: "Take Berlichingen along and measure his clothes, he shall be my squire." The Markgraf intended to leave as early as possible, but the Pfalzgraf[35] Philip arrived and he therefore had to remain there for two days longer. The Pfalzgraf planned to capture the Neumark and the Oberpfalz, because the Herzog Otto of Bavaria had just passed away.[36] I was appointed to be his squire and had to wait in his chambers. The next day the Pfalzgraf began his journey. This was an entire day after the Markgraf began his march with a third cohort. By the time we arrived in Oberlingen, the Swiss had already defeated one cohort. We therefore remained in Oberlingen for a while. After this, the troops of the Kaiser and

---

[34] Lasting from January to September of 1499, also known as the Swabian War. The rebellious Swiss confederacy, made up of a number of independent local governments, would effectively break away from the Empire with their victory over the Swabian League in 1499.

[35] Eng. "Count Palatine" or "Palsgrave," a high-ranking Count similar in status to the aforementioned *"Markgraf"* and *"Landgraf."* Historically, a non-hereditary position granted by the Emperor, but by Götz' time a prestigious hereditary title. The term usually, and in this case, refers to the Count Palatine of the Rhine, one of the seven Imperial Electors in the HRE.

[36] The Counts Palatine of the Rhine and the Dukes of Bavaria, members of the von Wittelsbach family, were involved in a perennial dynastic struggle that was not fully resolved until Napoleon's conquests on the Rhine and the subsequent mediatization of the various German principalities.

of the Reichsstädte[37] reorganized their troops and marched on with full force against Konstanz. The Kaiser joined us on this night. He wore an old green garment and a big green hat to avoid capture or identification. Despite my youth I easily recognized him by his nose, because I had visited many Reichstage with my uncles where I had seen him with my own eyes. The Kaiser had a good plan on his mind. During the night we arrived with the entire army on horseback and on foot near Konstanz. In the morning all cohorts were made ready and all horsemen and footmen were organized properly in the common fashion. The Kaiser and Markgraf Friedrich stuck together during all of this, along with many advisors and captains. I carried a long lance for my master, which was painted black and white. The flag on it was also black and white, and I wore a helmet with a grand feather plume of the same colors. As soon as the Kaiser saw me, he rode away from the Markgraf and asked me to whom I belonged. I said to him "To my dearest Prince and Master, Markgraf Friedrich." He then spoke: "You have a long spear and a large flag upon it. Ride to your cohort and remain with them until the Imperial Eagle-Banner[38] is raised above Konstanz." I followed his instructions, because I knew that he was the Kaiser and I would never doubt his orders. I arrived next to the Imperial Cupbearer,[39] Christoph von Limburg, who at this time had business with Nellenburg in Hagenau. After around half an hour, they gave the Cupbearer Christoph von Limburg the Imperial flag. It was the first and the last time I saw the Imperial Eagle fly on the field. I then went back to my Master and remained there for the rest of my service.

What my master and many others told my young seventeen-year-old noble self, is that we would have surprised and beaten

---

[37] Eng. "Free Imperial Cities," incorporated municipalities of high standing granted generous civic rights by the Emperor including representation in the *Riechstag*.
[38] The two-headed eagle, symbol of Imperial authority.
[39] A title of honor in many European noble courts.

the Swiss in Schwaderloch[40] if we had marched out on that day. We were supposed to break camp the next day, but a message arrived that the Swiss had received reinforcements and fortified themselves in advantageous positions. Because of this, the entire army was delayed. If we had attacked in the early days like the Kaiser had in mind, then we surely would have been in the advantageous position. Where there are many minds and too many advisors, often things do not go as they are supposed to. This has even happened in my own adventures.

Shortly after the Württembergian troops and the captains of the Markgraf with their cavalry and infantry led an army against Schaffhausen, we arrived near a place named Taingen, not far from Schaffhausen. A bunch of Swiss troops sat in a church tower and defended themselves, but did not want to surrender and instead said they would rather die like honorable oath-keepers.[41] Sir Melchior Süzel, who was defending the area between Schaffhausen and Taingen, was struck in the face with a stone by a group of Swiss soldiers who sallied out from the church. Many other nobles and non-nobles, on horse and on foot, where shot by the ones defending the church. When my horse, on which I served as a squire for the Markgraf, was shot, I ran on foot to the troops at the church and armed myself with an old spear because my rapier was still on the saddle of my dead horse. Suddenly Mister Jacob, a gunsmith and a thin little man, who stood bravely next to me, was hit with a shot. The round went through his body and hit another Württembergian man who had only thin armor; he was killed but the gunsmith survived. Finally, Sebaldus Spät and some others brought gunpowder and lit it under the church tower so that the soldiers inside burned alive. One Swiss soldier fell down from above with a child in his arms. The Swiss soldier perished, but the child walked away without harm. A knight of

---

[40] The forest near Konstanz.
[41] Swiss soldiers were renowned across Europe for their steadfast discipline.

the Markgraf took this child in. Where this child is today, I cannot tell, because I have not seen him since. Some knights spent too much time in the church, perhaps to pillage, but the powder caught up to them and they burned miserably in the fire. I cannot know if they all died or some survived, but nobody walked out. Our cohort on foot and horseback expected the enemy to attack while we ran out of the church, but nothing occurred and so we left. I did not participate in any serious fights during this war besides that situation. I also do not know anything special about the Swiss wars beyond that. Our enemies defeated many Imperial cohorts, but my Markgraf was not among the defeated. Also, Graf[42] Heinrich of Fürstenberg was overrun in his camp in Sundgau during the night and defeated. Only two men out of his army escaped and made it to the camp of the Markgraf. Heinrich himself and most of his troops were captured. Because of those two, I learned how this all could have happened. They talked about all the carelessness, clumsiness and cowardice that caused this failure. I stood next to the Markgraf on the night when he received the unfortunate news.

---

[42] A Count of no particular distinction, outranked by Dukes or other Counts of Ducal stature.

Part III

One year after this I started wearing armor again[43]; the story goes like this: My brother Philip and I rode to Heilbronn to visit our dear wives, around halfway through Lent time. When we were on our way home again and rode through Neustadt near Kocher, a man ran after us, whose name was Hans the Black, and yelled out for us. I noticed him first and said to my brother: "He is running after us and yells, let us hear what he wants!" We therefore stopped until he caught up to us. He told us that a good man had requested us to join as riders in his service. I responded by asking in what state this man was; if he was such a good man, then why did he not come himself and ask us? We gave him a letter and went on our way. The next day the man arrived in Jagsthausen. It was the old Thalacker,[44] who was the enemy of the Herzog of Württemberg. He asked us to provide him with three horses. He then gave my brother a horse, and I enlisted two servants as horsemen as well, to aid his cause.[45] He himself had only three armed guards, among them a man named Hasselschwerd[46] and another friend, so that we were all together six men. We started by capturing eleven rich Württembergian peasants on the Kapfenhard near Heilbronn, because the weekly market was on this day in the city. Thalacker meant to ransom them on St. George's Day[47] in Treuenfels. We then rode onward to

---

[43] A common saying at the time, meaning to get oneself in trouble or instigate conflict.
[44] Thalacker von Massenbach, an infamous Swabian brigand who had made a fortune looting and ransoming his way across Southern Germany.
[45] That is, to help him wage war against the Duke of Württemberg.
[46] Likely a *Nom de Guerre*, from the South German *Hascherl* (poor, unfortunate) and *Schwert* (sword), which together suggest an occupation as a brigand or hedge-knight.
[47] April 23rd

Heilbronn, took hold of everything and everyone that was Württembergian, and dared ourselves even to the walls of the city, in full sight of the guards on the wall. It was the first time I wore full knights' armor. Before then I only served as a junior noble or as a squire. I joined the bunch of knights and footmen I mentioned earlier and made many acquaintances with them over the two years while also growing attached to them. Later on, Thalacker's bunch became an enemy of the entire League.[48]

After these two years, I rode towards Sodenberg to my relative Master Neidhard von Thüngen to collect a horse which he had promised me. I arrived at this residence and could not find him. When he arrived, he ordered clothes to be tailored for me and asked that I should stay with him. Because he was my mother's brother, I could not bring myself to decline his invitation and remained the entire winter with him. I believe he wanted me to stay with him to keep me away from Thalacker's bunch, where I could have easily ended up dead. When spring arrived, trouble started between the Markgraf of Ansbach and the people of Nuremberg. As soon as I heard of this, I was ready to ride out along with the Markgraf and four horses without demanding any pay. The Markgraf raised me up as a squire. I was therefore obliged to aid him as well as I could, like a young man should in such situations. I did my part so well, without any desire for praise or fame, that the Markgraf sent his man Casimir to tell me, in only the best intentions, that he did not request such service of me, and that I did not need to stick so close to him. I therefore gave the most honorable Markgraf a very sharp response. I think that I said, "I am here to ride. If one demanded that of me, and if I did not ride, then the most honorable Markgraf would also not be pleased." After I told him I was ready to leave if he just wanted

---

[48] Almost certainly referring to the Swabian League, an Imperial-sponsored alliance of South German princes in which the Duchy of Württemberg played a key part. The League played a major part in the Imperial campaigns previously described, later disbanding as the Protestant Reformation divided its members along confessional lines.

the horses, he replied that I was riding along without any orders anyway. He was not wrong about this. Any time twenty or thirty horsemen wanted to ride out I volunteered to ride with them, because I was there for that purpose anyway. I got no profit from this undertaking, besides the quartermaster giving me more food for my readiness.

Captain Paul von Absberg took me in after this so that I could stand by his side in the field. We got along very poorly.[49] The troops of the Markgraf were ordered to break camp during the night. The Markgraf's foot soldiers had already marched ahead bravely. In the middle of night, we arrived in Schwabach. Mister Sigmund von Lentersheim and myself were the first at the gate. When the entire army was assembled, we marched on and after a march of around half a mile Christoph von Gieg with his knights joined us. He stayed on guard for the entire night. I knew he would grab this pig by the ears, because he was not fond of Nuremberg and had already been enemies with them previously. I tried to stick with Christoph von Gieg when all cohorts on horseback and on foot were set up in their positions, but my good Master Paul von Absberg noticed this. He recognized me by my armor and shouted two or three times: "Christoph! Christoph!" Christoph von Gieg then asked what he wanted of him and the man from Absberg shouted: "Leave the one from Berlichingen here and take my kinsman Hans Georg von Absberg with you instead." I therefore remained with my Captain. The Master of Absberg tried to gain an advantage by marching through the water ditch towards Nuremberg to scout out their positions and fortifications. To our surprise, the Nurembergians were prepared with a large force and cannons, and sent one shot after another into our lines. Von Absberg and his troops retreated, in a mad dash to get away as fast as possible. We could not take good cover inside the forest. The Nurembergians were putting so much

---

[49] Literally translated, Götz writes "We wanted to invite each other to the church," a sarcastic way of saying that they wanted to fight each other.

pressure on us with their cannons and wagon forts[50] that we could not remain anywhere for a long time, because no one particularly enjoys getting shot at. We then arrived at the area where the Markgraf was waiting with his formation of cavalry and infantry for the enemy to arrive. It was near the city, not far from the forest around Nuremburg, which gave them the advantage and put us in a tight spot. Our strength was around seven hundred cavalrymen, together with footmen numbering around three hundred Landsknechts and three hundred Swiss pikemen. When the time felt right for them, the Nurembergians started marching towards us with their cannon, their wagon forts, and their foot-soldiers together. They truly were not unprepared, but appeared to have trained their cannons and wagon forts well. When both sides collided, we and our captains sent messengers to Markgraf Casimir asking his grace to support us. It was urgently needed and the enemy had the advantage, requiring our full attention. Markgraf Casimir responded by telling us to keep going and in God's name, he would reinforce us and be with us soon like a brave prince should. We held position in God's name, but all of the Markgraf's infantry fell back besides the cohort of Kitzinger, which remained with us and the three hundred Landsknechts, three hundred Swiss footmen, and the remaining cavalry. With this force we pushed towards the enemy, but the shots of the enemy cannon hit in such mass that we could barely see each other through the smoke. When we got to the wagon fort, they were almost able to close it up, coming quite close through the efforts of the quite talented waggoneers. An instinct then arose in my heart, or was

---

[50] The use of wagons as mobile fortifications was pioneered by the anti-Catholic Hussite forces in Bohemia (modern Czechia) during the Hussite Wars (1419–1434). The tactic involved the use of multiple wagons to create a continuous circle from which crossbow- or gunpowder-equipped infantry could fire down at an attacking force with impunity, while preventing enemy cavalry from getting inside their formation. Evidently, the tactic was still in use by some forces in Götz' time, and notably used later by Boer and American settlers (hence the American expression "circling the wagons").

perhaps inspired by God. It compelled me to slay the horse from under the lead rider of the wagon fort. Thereby I prevented the others from moving forward, compelling them to halt. I then, without any directives or orders from the captains, stopped the enemy from closing the gap between the wagons. The delay I caused against the enemy was a great advantage for us, and surely was not insignificant for our good fortune and victory. I, for one, do not know how this battle could have turned out any other way if not for my actions.[51] The enemy was strong, and had cannons and the wagon fort in position. They were rested and we were tired; enemy reinforcements were on the way and were already so close that were already skirmishing with them. Against those reinforcements we lost most our cavalry, because we first thought they were our allies until their cannons opened fire and put many troops of our cohort to flight. Those reinforcements I beat myself, together with Sir Hans Hund, captain of the Markgraf's cavalry, or else we would surely have been captured. We fought so bravely that the enemy was forced again to retreat. This was our luck, because when the Nurembergians saw their injured troops fleeing from us they realized that they had lost the battle and that their army was beaten. We still lost many brave men. I considered myself dead at one point because my horse was heavily injured, and it later died of the same injury. Additionally, it was such a hot day that more people were strangled by the heat than were killed by weapons. At first I thought the heat I felt was only from exertion and the close formation, but I was later informed that the heat in those days had been exceptional in any case. We therefore captured the battlefield, took their cannons and

---

[51] Wagon-forts were very effective, but vulnerable if an attacker could move quickly enough to prevent the waggoneers from securely linking them together. This would allow the attacking force to get inside the defensive line and engage the crossbowmen, gunners, and artillery up close. While perhaps not obvious to a modern reader, if Götz' claim of single-handedly preventing the wagons from being linked is true, he may well have turned the tide of the battle with his quick action.

wagon fort, and marched with them to the camp in Schwabach. Later I saw the captured guns again in the armory near Ansbach and even saw an iron culverin[52] which I recognized from that battle.

This battle occurred on a Sunday after the St. Vitus' Day[53] in the year 1502. Right the next day, I went from my residence near Schwabach to another inn where we often ate. On my way there, I spotted a little man sitting on a long wooden log. He was called Hänschen, from Eberstadt in the Weinsberger Valley, and I felt like I knew him. "Hänschen," I said, "is that you?" and when he responded with "yes," I asked him where he was from. To my astonishment, he then said that he was from Nuremberg. I instantly asked him with the words: "What hassle and trouble was going on in the city yesterday?" He responded, "Mercenaries, such a terror has not been heard or seen in a long time." I asked him, "Why?" "No man remained at his post or at the gates, and the fleeing ones were pushing against the gates in such a panic that many fell into the moat. The bridges of the city were brought down, and they then ran towards the castle and the other gates." He spoke the truth, and I heard the same account from other people thereafter, even from citizens of Nuremburg themselves that I captured later, after the manner of this Hans von Eberstadt. He also told me that when they saw their own men fleeing, they thought that we, that is, their enemies, must have seen it too. Considering the circumstances, this does not seem unlikely to me either. But dear God! We were already tired and had worked hard to capture the cannons and their wagon forts and bring them to our camp. We would have surely captured Nuremburg if we would have kept going and had not been so

---

[52] The culverin (Fr. *Couleuvrine* or Ger. *Feldschlange,* both meaning "field snake") was a small-caliber cannon that could shoot more precisely over longer ranges than the larger and heavier bombard or houfnice. Its name is suggestive of its place as a lighter support weapon used by the infantry in a direct-fire role.
[53] June 15th

exhausted. Both my brother and I participated in this war without any pay, and also never demanded such, because we had freely volunteered. Right after this though, a great assembly happened near Ansbach between the von Thüngens and the von Heßbergs, who owned the new castle where I did squire duties for my relative Master Neidhard von Thüngen. On that day, both had the best knights and soldiers in all of Franconia, and Georg von Rosenberg[54] was also there. An argument occurred around this time in the inn named "Haken,"[55] between him and Captain Paul von Absberg. The topic was the battle described earlier, and Georg von Rosenberg told him: "My dear Markgraf had many loyal and good men with him on this day, and where one has such men, one can also strike well at the enemy." The captain responded, "Yes, my Lord had brave men, but I saw no braver men than the two Berlichingen brothers." I do not think that Mister von Absberg was aware that I was in the room. As I stood there, I shoved a fellow comrade with my arm and said "Do you hear what he is saying?" He responded "Yes." I indeed knew of no Berlichingens who fought in this battle on that day besides my brother Philipp and myself. My relative Bernhard only arrived after eight days in Schwabach, and was not in the battle.

This was worth more to me and my dearest brother than if the Markgraf would have gifted us two thousand gulden,[56] even though we were poor fellows. It was payment enough that not only the Markgraf but also the highest advisors, captains, knights and soldiers gave us honors, praise and glory. Even the ones thirty miles away from us still spoke well of us, at least from what friends told us. This was more valuable to us than gold or silver, which we would not have accepted anyway. When I went to ride home, only one out of the four horses I had

---

[54] An infamously quarrelsome knight, known for fighting many duels and especially for his feuds with Bishop Rudolf of Schwerenberg.

[55] "The Hook"

[56] German gold coinage based on the Italian Florin, known in England as the "Guilder."

in the battle remained. It was the wildest one, but the Markgraf's advisors generously gave me some of their own personal horses. Especially worth mentioning is Sir Veit von Vestenberg, who gave me his dearest horse. This was a surprise to everyone, because they believed that even if the Markgraf himself begged for it, von Vestenberg would not have given it freely. This pay, like I said, was for me and my brother the most valuable thing imaginable, and we were happy even if we remained the poorest fellows of the nobility.

Part IV

After the battle at Nuremburg which, like I described, happened on the Sunday after St. Vitus' Day, I rode off with Neidhard von Thüngen, who I waited for on Michaelmas[57] down at the Sodenberg.[58] We met two riders on the way around a small wood near the village of Obereschenbach. They were Eindriß von Gemünd, Amtmann[59] of Saaleck, and his squire, who had the nickname "the Affe."[60] Before I arrived at Sir Neidhard's residence, there had been a big meeting near Hammelburg, where my relative Graf Wilhelm of Henneberg and Graf Michael of Wertheim were present. In this meeting, the troubles with the enemy, the earlier mentioned Michael von Wertheim, had been discussed and settled. When I one day had gone to visit the inn where Sir Neidhard and his men usually were, most often in a drunken state, I found the Affe there as well. He was very full, both of himself and of alcohol, and made many boasts and speeches. He said "What does this young master[61] want here, does he also want to belong to us?" and other demeaning phrases, with which he tried to get on my nerves. This made me quite bitter and I responded: "What do I care about your rude speech and your drunkenness? When we meet on the battlefield, we will see who is the master and who is the servant!" Now then, when we came down the Sodenberg,

---

[57] Celebrated on September 29th in the Western world, or October 10th/11th on the old calendar.

[58] A mountain in Franconia, connected to a local tradition identifying it as the resting place of Noah's Ark after the Flood.

[59] Equivalent to the English "Bailiff," the highest-ranking retainer of a territorial lord, responsible for administration of the estates, collection of taxes, enforcement of laws, etc.

[60] German for "ape" or "monkey."

[61] The original term, *Junker*, literally denotes a young nobleman, and had not yet acquired its connection to the Prussian nobility.

I thought to myself, "that's the Affe with his master!" I instantly made for some high ground, loading my crossbow from the saddle as I rode across a long track. His master rode to the village to rile the farmers up. The Affe also had a crossbow but ran away like his master. When I was right behind him, he had to run into the ditch which led towards the village, and I still had quite a way to go until I would have reached the spot where the ditch led to. Therefore, I let him run into the ditch, and shot him in the back. I instantly wanted to reload my crossbow because he also had a bolt on his, but I decided not to do so. I expected him to try to ambush me and therefore kept after him. He noticed my crossbow was not loaded and awaited me near the gate until I drew close. He shot at me and hit my chest armor, so that the bolt split apart and flipped over my head. I instantly threw my crossbow at his throat because I still had no bolt in it, drew my sword and struck him to the ground, laying his horse's nose in the dirt. But he got back on his legs and begged the farmers to help him. As I was hunting him through the village, I noticed a farmer who had already put a bolt on his crossbow. I jumped on him and beat him before he had a chance to fire. I held my sword back, grabbed him and told him I belonged to Neidhard von Thüngen and that we were friends of Fulda.[62] During this an entire mob of farmers came at me and encircled me. They had boar-spears, hand-axes, throwing-axes, wood-axes, and stones. "Nothing thrown, nothing kept! Nothing struck, nothing gained!" the farmers shouted as their clubs and stones flew past and into my head, ringing my helmet like a bell. As I was running away, a farmer came at me with his spear and slashed my arm so hard it felt like it was cut in two. When I tried to stab him with my sword, he ducked under my horse so that I couldn't lean far enough over to hit him. I still broke through the mob, and while doing so gave a farmer who carried a

---

[62] The Princely Abbey of Fulda, ruled by a Catholic abbot as an ecclesiastical principality, controlled the territory on which these events took place.

wooden club such a strike that he smashed against a fence. My horse was by now exhausted and didn't want to keep going anymore, and this had me worried about how I would get out the gate. I hurried ahead just as someone tried to close it, but I managed to get out just before it shut. The Affe was waiting outside with four farmers next to him, and shouted "Come Closer! Come Closer!" shooting at me so that I saw the bolt fly and skim across the grass. I charged at him and scared all five of them back into the village. The farmers now charged back at me but I rode hastily away. When I finally met up with Sir Neidhard again, who was away near a field, some of the farmers stared after us, but no one was brave enough to come any closer. Right when I arrived near Neidhard, one farmer came with his plow raised and was shouting a battle cry. I caught him and made him beg for his life. He swore that he was only trying to return my crossbow, which I had thrown after the Affe and had no time to pick up again.

Part V

In the year 1503 I served with Thalacker's gang, together with friends and comrades again. For fourteen days we had to hide inside a forest, but we had friends and charitable people who brought us cheese and bread so that we could sustain ourselves. Thalacker's bunch had good men, friends, and donors everywhere, so we always had a place to hide. My brother and I also aided them by giving them advice and information whenever we could. This did not always save them though, and they had poor luck in some places. When we left one such bad place with two of Thalacker's riders, it happened that we came across some hostile men. This happened so quickly that neither we nor the enemy could load their crossbows. One of Thalacker's riders, named Hasselschwerd, and his companion always rode with their crossbows drawn, so they only had to put their bolts in them. I began to charge at a rider who also, like myself, didn't have his crossbow loaded, and crossed swords with him. I successfully smashed his sword and crossbow away so that he was unarmed. One of these enemies was fighting my companion and attempted to flee, so I jumped in front of him and got him to stand still. He had a short rapier with which he wounded both of the Thalackers without giving them any chance to strike him in return. I rode towards them and told them to make sure the one I defeated alone could not flee, and to leave the last one to me. He tried to flee but I caught up to him and put my sword into his horse, stopping both. It was then obvious to both sides what a bad situation our enemies put themselves in, but I held myself back. We were good knights and not greedy, but good-willing. The Thalacker men also left after this, God only knows to where.

Part VI

In the year 1504 the Bavarian War began. Before this war, Pfalzgraf Philipp of Heidelberg marched up to Würzburg and thence into Bavaria. His intent was possibly to conquer it, because Herzog Georg had just passed away. Herzog Georg had inherited all of Bavaria to him, if I remember correctly.[63] First, he reunited with Graf Michael in Wertheim, who then marched with him towards Würzburg. Two Counts of the Pfalzer faction,[64] Graf Bernhard of Solms and a Graf of Isenburg, had just left the city and were ready to go home. Kunz Schott[65] was also inside Würzburg, but wanted to oppose the Pfalzgraf, and rode with Neidhard von Thüngen out of the city. Master Neidhard put his troops under my command, so that I could serve Kunz Schott, who at this time was not a knight yet and not an enemy of the Pfalzer faction, but it was clear to me where his sympathies lay. Not a single nobleman was among the troops given to me, besides myself and Götz von Thüngen. Kunz Schott loaned me his best horse right before we marched into the battlefield and even gave me command of his riders. I told him that I had a good horse myself and that I could have even spared some of my own troops, but in the end, he insisted, and I had to ride on his horse. I also resisted his offer to put some of his troops under my command. Personally, I would

---

[63] Herzog Georg of Bavaria-Landshut left his lands to his daughter, who was married to Ruprecht, son and heir of Pfalzgraf Philipp of the Palatinate. In response, Herzog Albrecht of Bavaria-Munich made an alliance with the Kaiser and other powerful rulers to press his claim to the inheritance of Landshut. This conflict was part of the larger pattern of Wittelsbach dynastic disputes (*See* fn. 29).

[64] That is, supporters of Ruprecht.

[65] Konrad "Kunz" Schott was another prolific South German knight and mercenary, commander of Rothenburg Castle, and habitual enemy of the Free City of Nuremberg.

have preferred them to serve under someone more experienced in this matter, because he had with him very capable men who had served previously under the Pfalzgraf and the Landgraf. In the end, he insisted on this order, and the troops had to follow my command. I met up with my relative Götz von Thüngen and we stuck together for a long time. He had one man with him who knew the paths and fields very well (or so I would learn a quarter of a year later), which should have given us an advantage, but this did not help much at all. When the route led below the mountains, we had to walk on footpaths, but I was of the opinion that it was not in our favor to remain at the bottom and climbed up. Fresh snow had just fallen on the path so one could spot hoof prints. I spotted the fresh marks on the snow, like we expected, and we even saw the spit of the horses. I notified Konrad Schott of my discovery and concluded from all the fresh spit that they could not be far from us, which turned out to be true. Konrad Schott was a lazy rider though, and did not want to remain in the Spessart,[66] even after riding just barely three miles. With a great deal of insistence, I could motivate him to march as far as the next Thuringian village. We therefore did not accomplish anything at that time.

During this earlier-mentioned year, in which the Bavarian war started, I remained with my relative Neidhard von Thüngen. It was against my will that I had to march with him into Bavaria, because my two brothers were on the Pfalzgrafian side and I would have greatly preferred to be with them. I rode with my relative to the Markgraf, who was in Roth with his troops. We conquered Hilpoltstein and some other territories in the Oberpfalz. The Nurembergians rapidly collected their troops when the Markgraf sent out his men, both on horseback and on foot, towards the Oberpfalz. He himself rode first with the cavalry towards Ingolstadt, then to Munich towards Herzog Albrecht, where the Imperial and League

---

[66] A range of low wooded mountains, on the border between the modern German states of Bavaria and Hesse.

troops regrouped. The Markgraf started marching from there with some of his troops towards Landau and captured it. Georg von Rosenberg was defending this city with his guards and some Bohemians and held it for quite some time, all while taking cannon shots, even though it was not very fortified. We then also captured Braunau and marched towards Landshut. We had more confrontations and skirmishes than can be retold. The two hardest fights were before Landshut on a Saturday and a Sunday, where I was wounded by a gunshot. My dear friends and the Markgraf pressured the honorable Master and Ruler, Herzog Ruprecht, to allow me free passage to Landshut, so I could heal there. I remained in the camp before Landshut on the day of the injury for a night. Early the cool morning (It was very hot in those damned days, especially for someone who has just been injured so gravely) I marched on and was supposed to be placed in the residence of Sigmund von Thüngen, and from there to go on to my relatives. But early in the morning, when we started leaving the camp near Landshut, Christoph von Gieg, who was on Ruprecht's side and had guard duty on this night, started riding towards us. The march-leader therefore came to a halt, and allowed our pursuer to ride up to our wagon-fort. As soon as Christoph von Gieg learned that I had been shot, he ordered me brought to his own residence, because of how we had come to know one another during the earlier battle at Nuremberg. I therefore came into the residence of Christoph von Gieg rather than into the residence of my relatives. He did many good deeds for me and explained that I was welcome to stay for as long as I wished. If I desired or wanted anything, he would do everything in his power to get it for me. He also informed me, "I still have money of which my comrades do not know, and if they knew of it, they would not give me any peace and quiet." He told me the amount and said: "I don't want to keep it secret from you." Many other friends also visited me, such that I could not have any peace for three days. It felt like a pilgrimage was occurring towards the residence. Many acquaintances came to see how I was doing, including Georg von Rosenberg, Truchseß[67] Georg von Aue, and many others of the highest nobility. They told me that the charitable Herzog Ruprecht had pity for me even though I was on the opposing side of the battlefield. Yes, a good friend even came by to tell me to wear nice and clean clothing because he heard Herzog Ruprecht himself would come by to visit. I did, and waited for him, but the news started going around that his grace had fallen sick in the Ruhr region and had passed away. Christoph von Gieg and many others also died of the same disease around this time. The Almighty Lord took many in a short while in this sorrowful place; meanwhile my sickness did not end so abruptly.

Here is how my injury occurred. I acted as a young fellow, full of manly courage, and thinking that while I was young I ought to make myself a man in good company. On Sunday near Landshut, we were fighting a battle like I described earlier, and the Nurembergians aimed a cannon at friend and foe alike. Our enemies had an advantageous position in a ditch, and I would have very much desired to clash my spear against them. When I was standing still and was looking for an opportunity to strike, the Nurembergians suddenly turned their cannon against us, and with it shot my sword pommel in two, so that half of it cut into my arm and into the bracers too. The pommel was so deep in the bracers that one could not see it anymore. It still surprises me that I did not fall off my horse. My bracers stayed whole, besides the corners, which stood out a bit. The other parts of the sword grip were not split into two, but I could not see them. I think those parts were the ones that cut my hand off, between the glove and the crossbow-gear. The arm was shattered from front to back. When I noticed that my hand hung limply by the skin and my spear dropped below my horse, I acted like nothing happened. I turned my horse around, and got away from the enemy and back to my people without any

---

[67] Equivalent to the English "Seneschal," a senior retainer or steward in charge of a noble household, often an honorific title.

trouble. An old Landsknecht came to me who wanted to join the battle. I called him over and asked him to stay with me, because he saw how dire my situation was. He did as I said and then left to find the doctor. When I arrived in Landshut, my old comrades, who fought against me in this battle, described to me how I was shot. A nobleman named Fabian von Wallsdorf, a Vogtlander, was hit by the same shot and was killed by it even though the shot hit me first, therefore both friend and enemy were harmed by it. This nobleman was a fine, beautiful man, so beautiful you could not find a more handsome man among a thousand men.

I was also told what I did on Saturday and Sunday and they gave me all the details, from what armor I wore to which horse I rode. They also knew all my actions in detail. I remained in Landshut from St. Jacob's Day[68] until Carnival[69] and I do not need to mention what great pains I felt during that time. I begged God to be merciful and take me up to him because I was now a ruined warrior. I then remembered a knight who I had heard of from my father, old Pfalzgrafs, and Hohenlohian[70] knights. His name was Köchli. He also had only one hand and still could do everything he needed to do against his enemies on the battlefield, like everyone else. I prayed to God and thought to myself that even if I had twelve hands, they would be useless if I did not have His grace. My iron hand[71] was only a minor benefit, but I still wanted to be as capable on the battlefield as any other normal man. I rode with Köchli's sons

---

[68] July 15th

[69] A time of feasting before Lent begins, recognized as Mardi Gras in France and other countries.

[70] The Hohenlohe were a South German princely dynasty of respectable stature.

[71] Götz does not mention his namesake iron prosthetic in detail. The initial prosthetic was crude, and he later had a second, more elegant one made by expert German craftsmen. The second hand was quite impressive even by modern standards, and could be adjusted to hold reins, a lance, or even something as small and precise as a quill pen. The iron hands still exist, and are kept on display at the castle museum in Jagsthausen.

thereafter, who were famous and charismatic riders. I truly cannot speak any more misfortune of this accident after having fought for almost sixty years with only one fist in wars, feuds, and troubles. God in His mercy truly gave me His grace in all of them.

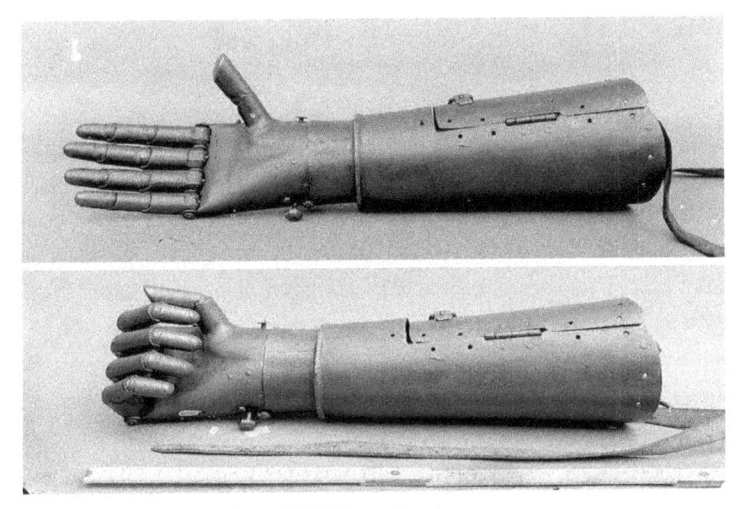

One of Götz' Iron Hands

More had come to pass in Bavaria. Our captains who belonged to St. George's Flag[72] at the time, Sir Neidhard von Thüngen and Sir Wilhelm the Marshal of Pappenheim held joint command of the forces, but rotated this position every day. One day a message was spread in the camp that two enemy cohorts were in Neuenmark, which was not far from Röttingen in Bavaria, and the captains said that whoever was in the mood to join the march against them could volunteer. I volunteered, and another hundred or 150 friendly and talkative comrades joined along. I knew we would stick together in life as in death. When we started marching through a big forest, around

---

[72] In the year of 1437 lords, counts, knights, and footmen of Swabia agreed to an alliance in honor of Sir Georg to uphold peace and stability in Swabia. The men of that alliance were called the "St. George's Flags."

evening, I was at the front of the march. I saw some people who were running away from us. I successfully went after them, caught two and restrained them. They were two peasants who had sided with the enemy. I had to hold onto them until the others arrived. One landowning troublemaker[73] came over, who was even more energetic than me. He held one of the peasants and started beating him horribly. Nobody was there to witness this besides me, the landowner and the peasants. I rode to him and asked bluntly what his business with this peasant was and why he beat him so badly. He responded condescendingly, so in response I punched him accordingly. Suddenly Georg von Frundsberg,[74] who was not yet a knight at this time, arrived with twenty or thirty riders and demanded that both of us swear peace. My enemy instantly swore off the dispute, but I did not want to do so, and told him: "Why do you beat my prisoners? Why do you not catch your own? If you dare to punch another prisoner, I shall not tolerate it." Georg von Frundsberg then started surrounding me with his knights. One had a bolt loaded onto his crossbow and the others were armed similarly. I was standing there like a wild pig,[75] but I did not want to swear peace and instead stuck to my story. It was almost night when I planned to just fight my way out of there as soon as they put a hand on me, but I did swear on my knight's honor that I would not do anything against the landowner unless he started it. If he did so again, I said I shall break his neck or he shall break mine. This proposal calmed them down. We marched on and arrived deep in the night in Braunau. The next morning a messenger was sent by Sir Georg

---

[73] Götz calls him an idiomatic insult, "Gecksnase," which literally translates to "lizard nose."

[74] A fellow Swabian and participant in the Swiss and Bavarian wars, Georg von Frundsberg is perhaps the most famous of the German Knights. He would later become the commander of the Imperial forces during the Italian Wars (1494–1559), organizing the Empire's professional infantry (the *Landsknechte*). Frundsberg gained his triumph with the capture of King Francis I of France at the Battle of Pavia in 1525.

[75] In reference to the then-popular sport of boar hunting.

and his crowd. I was supposed to come to them, and when I arrived, they all sat around and drank wine. They stole from the farmers and bought wine with their money. I therefore also took a swig and they invited me to sit along with them and to keep drinking on. I soon walked away and did not drink much more, because I had much to do. I tell this story because Sir Georg von Frundsberg and Franz von Sickingen liked me a lot. The people of Heilbronn once wanted to put me into a prison unbecoming of a knight, but both of them insisted that I was put into fitting prison for as long as I was forced to be there. I still have the paper of their demands in my possession. During the night they came into my room in the Ditz inn, so many of them that not all of them could find a place to sit and most of them had to stand. We fooled around and were merry. Suddenly, Sir Georg started thinking about the earlier mentioned loot, and said: "My dear Götz, do you remember when we acquired that loot in the Bavarian lands?" I responded, "Yes, obviously I remember it very well." He then said: "You wanted to become a Nessel[76] around that time." I did not want to start an argument with him, because he had been very chivalrous and calm before this. He was also always friendly to me after this.

After this it occurred that a certain Bohemian man became an enemy of the Bohemian crown. His name was Hans von Selbitz. Some other knights and I wanted to aid him and offer him our services. We scouted as soon as possible for the richest and most noble men who directed the affairs of the Bohemian crown (at this time a very young King sat on the throne who was not yet able to rule) who travelled through various paths. We discovered that they were from the Netherlands,[77] and we

---

[76] A nettle plant; idiomatically, a weakling or coward.
[77] At this point ruled by the Habsburgs as the "Austrian Netherlands," including Belgium and Luxemburg in addition to the modern territory of the Netherlands. "Netherlands" simply means "lowlands," and had not yet acquired its connection to the modern Republic. It was also sometimes referred to as "Lower Burgundy."

also knew that they were on their way back and that they directed the affairs of the Bohemian crown. I was ordered to ride down there with some knights who knew the area well, and I was allowed to choose the knights myself. We rode at least three to four weeks until we knew how and where we could get to them. They had hired guards and I was notified that they had started going in our direction. Philipp Sturmfeder wrote my brother and I that we should come to Heidelberg on a specific day, and should take friends with us to stay there for a couple of days. This we did. Hans von Selbitz, my brother Philipp, and others, among them the man who was the enemy of the Bohemian crown, rode into Heidelberg without being recognized. Many folks in the Hirsch inn did proudly show off their coats of arms, and so the foolish enemy of the Bohemian crown did so too, without our knowledge. When we finally arrived, ate and drank, the Bohemians had arrived too. They went for a walk around the market and when they looked over to us, they noticed the hung-up coats of arms. Among them was the one of their enemy. A big upheaval began among them and they ran to the Pfalzgraf and begged him for support. They were given knights and armor and headed out towards us. This is how the foolish little man ruined our plan through his coat of arms, so that we could do nothing. If this didn't happen it surely would have come to a good deal for all of us and they would have made peace. I cannot remember his name, but you can still find his coat of arms in the Hirsch inn in Heidelberg. I truly thought he was a capable and brave man, but thereafter I quickly realized that he was young and naïve, and made himself an enemy without being very skilled in such matters, but he did have good teachers around him. Later I learned that he made peace with the Crown of Bohemia.

A certain Ulrich Beck, a burgher[78] and livestock trader near Kitzingen, who at this time was a backbencher of Markgraf

---

[78] A member of the wealthy urban class, more commonly identified by the more modern French appellation "bourgeoisie."

Friedrich, was a wealthy man and had a wife who had previously been married to man from the Seyboth family. This woman had a son named Philipp, who became Neidhard von Thüringen's squire. Ulrich Beck, the stepfather, and Philip Seyboth, the stepson, right before he became an armed guard, requested that I aid them with arms and counsel against the Waldströmers, who sat in Nuremburg and were of nobility. The Waldströmers had harmed them over some inheritance troubles, and I was supposed to aid in finding a way to get their goods back if there was no peaceful way. I responded to their request like this: "My dear Lord, Markgraf Friedrich raised me, and if you want to go after your rightfully deserved goods by rightful means than I shall aid you with advice and action and I shall not lack any motivation in doing so." We then thought about this situation further and made a proposition that we capture the Waldströmers right after our agreement was settled, in the Nurembergian forest right when they went to visit their villages in the morning for church on St. Matthew's Day.[79] They were two brothers; one of them had a pretty young son along with him, who politely asked us to spare him, which we did. We took the two brothers along and marched day and night until we arrived in Jagsthausen. The advisors of the Markgraf got involved and called us and the Waldströmers to Ansbach. I marched along as a helping hand with some friends. The Markgraf took the side of the Waldströmers, by claiming that they were his servants. This was not fully wrong. They did hereditary service on a number of the Markgraf's lands around Nuremberg. Even though Ulrich Beck was the Markgrafs backbencher and the Waldströmers were his servants, the advisors somehow managed to reach an agreement between the two and achieved peace. What benefits I accrued from this situation, I now forget. Ulrich Beck certainly gave me something, but I cannot remember what or how much it was. I already reported on this story once before, so I did not want to

---

[79] September 21st

leave that part unmentioned, especially because the aforementioned Philipp Seyboth was my relative's squire and servant.

Part VII

After the Bavarian Wars, many nobles and brave knights, I among them, were requested by a man they named "the Mutineer."[80] He was the enemy of Rothenburg. My relative Willibald von Thüngen opened his residence on the Reußenberg[81] to him. We offered him our services and did one or two knightly tasks for him. The capable Lord and Master, Bishop Lorenz of Würzburg, took the matter into his own hands and achieved an agreement between both parties even though my men and I wanted to keep working for the man. We even insisted on it, and the letters were already written, but through God's help and the pious bishop's meddling, the situation was put to rest and we were not required anymore.

---

[80] A somewhat-infamous troublemaker from Rothenburg. He was executed by sword in the year 1513.
[81] A number of similarly-named locations are possible, but most probable is the Reußenberg region near Schwäbish Hall in Wurttemberg.

Part VIII

The next year, many of my good friends at the court of Herzog Ulrich of Württemberg, especially my brother-in-law Reinhard von Saxonheim, came to me for a request from a man named Hans Sindelfinger. He was a tailor by trade. He was a magnificent marksman[82] and was born in Stuttgart. He won a shooting competition and received the highest prize in Cologne, around one hundred gulden if I remember correctly. But the Cologners cheated him out of his prize and did not want to pay him. He sued for his money through the noble court. My brother-in-law Reinhard von Saxonheim wrote me in his court's name and asked of me to support the man's cause. This I did, and became Cologne's enemy and captured two merchants, father and son. Right after these, nine wagons were coming up from Frankfurt, which were also from Cologne. I stormed at them myself, but my knights and footmen were not far away. I rode up to Kronberg about this matter to get the permission and advice of the Marshal in Heidelberg to lead the wagons to Kronberg. This took a while because he was old and sick, and I did not want to give him more troubles. The Master of Königstein was also very fond of me, so I did not want to attack the wagons on his road, but chose a different one which was near his border. I sent a footman named Sinterus to him with the notification that I had spared his grace and was ready to attack the wagons in another place. I did so because I had great trust in the Graf and it would come back against me if my actions caused trouble for him. He let me know through my own footman, for his honor's sake, to not attack the wagons and urged me strongly to let them pass. He even offered to reward me in another way and set up a meeting between myself and

---

[82] The original idiom used is "pipeshooter."

the Cologners in Frankfurt, where this feud was finally settled.

I shall now describe what happened with the two earlier mentioned merchants I captured: One of them begged me to send him off to Leipzig, where he stored his goods, because in his current state, he could not help me or himself. I allowed him to do this but kept his son, because the father was old and I thought his son would bear the imprisonment better. I gave him a written contract and gave him instructions on how he had to behave. I truly expected he would uphold his written promise, both for my and his son's sake. I gave him the instruction that he should join up with the merchants of Nuremberg or whomever, and march out of Leipzig towards Coburg or Bamberg, because those were the safest routes. I gave him a young man who was under my command, along with my handwritten notice, included him in my promises, and swore that he could use my residences. If he saw one of my men while in possession of my notice, he could rest assured that he only had to follow him to be reunited with his son, or that his son would be sent to him. Before that I introduced the young man to him, who also explained to him the entire situation. He sadly became disloyal to me and to his own son and got my man arrested by the Bishop of Bamberg, who was named Georg von Limburg. I could have waited a long time, but the young man who I sent along acted more cleverly than I could have ever expected. It happened like this: I once rode with him out of Neustadt on the Aisch, past Hochstedt, which was owned by the Bishop of Bamberg. A nice spot in the forest was near. I told the young man, not thinking anything of it, that this was a nice place to rest. I told him about this, so that he would know of it once he became a rider himself. The young man remembered this. When I sent him to Bamberg, to the residence where the merchant was located and where, like I earlier mentioned, he was betrayed, captured and jailed, they asked him where I was located and where they could meet me. He then responded by mentioning the spot in the forest I told him about. My men and I were wearing black at the time, because my mother had passed away only three days before this. They therefore put another young man in black clothing and set him on the horse of my man and let him ride towards the forest. The Bambergian riders were behind him and thought they could find me there like my young man told them. But he was merely toying with them, and gave them a blind target, so they rode there for nothing. As soon as I was notified that my young man was incarcerated, I immediately wrote to the Bishop demanding that he shall release him without daring to ask any ransom, because I acted upon what was agreed upon in the contract, and reminded him of the talk we had in Schweinfurt about requesting riding services from me. I warned that if he did not release my man, then I would think of my own ways to free him. He delayed the matter from Pentecost to Michaelmas,[83] when the young man was supposed to be judged. During this, I learned that the bishop often went to Göppingen to the sour springs to aid against his stone disease.[84] I had the idea to ruin his bath and to remind him about my concerns. I was already prepared and hired multiple capable men for this venture. I gave an order to one man who I entrusted with everything, who even called himself "the mother of all riders,"[85] to hire some troops for me. But when he was hiring troops and one asked him for who, why and against whom he was hiring, he openly revealed my entire plan and may even have mentioned the bishop of Bamberg himself. This was truly not so smart of him. The person he told all this to, to motivate him to join our cause, then ran to the bishop at Göppingen and told him about our entire plan. We could not do anything then. If I had known that a betrayal was involved in all of this, then I would have surely attacked the bishop's brother, who would have quickly surrendered (but God didn't

---

[83] The seventh Sunday after Easter (late May or early June) to September 29th.
[84] "Stone disease" can have multiple meanings but, in this case, likely refers to a urinal infection.
[85] This is a literal translation, and probably has the same meaning one would understand it to have today.

seem to favor this). I rode from Jagsthausen towards Crailsheim near the Fils[86] to visit my friends from Rechberg. When I arrived in Swabia, I saw a lot of riders with their horses going through the fields and along the water ditches. I saw that they were wearing Bambergian colors. I told my troops to move on and that I would catch up with them soon. I then followed the ditch and greeted one of the riders and asked him who the horses belonged to. He responded: "They belong to the Cupbearer Friedrich von Limburg." This was the bishop's brother. At this time, I had no idea of the betrayal or that the bishop was warned about my plan, so I let the brother slide out of my hand and was therefore, as they say, stuck between two chairs.[87] I regretted it very strongly that I let this chance pass. Friedrich of Limburg was a good man. I would have not abducted him but instead jailed him in his own residence[88] until he could talk out a peace between his brother, the Bishop of Bamberg, and me. Even though I lost both of these opportunities, I still captured the bishop and a single knight of his in about eight to ten days and freed my young man again. Herzog Ulrich of Württemberg set an agreement up between the bishop and me, which laid this trouble to rest.

I once borrowed two men from my brother Philipp. They clashed one day with the sons of Philipp Stumpf,[89] with whom they had no prior business. Both were on foot. One of the sons was carrying a gun and the other one a spear. I do not want to say out loud what they were planning. One of the sons was only a half-Stumpf because his father had produced him with a maid. When they both met, like when people who have nothing to do with each other usually meet, my men told me they had nothing ill planned. They supposedly did not even have their crossbows drawn, or else they probably would have responded

---

[86] A small river near Göppingen.
[87] i.e., "between a rock and a hard place."
[88] In late Imperial feudal law, one noble could force another by oath to remain within his residence until an injustice was resolved.
[89] The Stumpfs were an old and distinguished Franconian noble family.

more cleverly. Then suddenly one of the Stumpf's started shooting his gun and hit one of my men through both of his arms. Now they had every right to respond appropriately to such an action. The heavily injured man threw down one of the Stumpfers even with his injuries. However, the one with the spear captured my brother Philipp's men. The testimonies of both of my men were taken and they were supposed to turn themselves in near Thomeneck in person. Sadly, they forgot their duty and did not show up. They lost their honor and became fugitives. If they would have shown up, I bet we would have been good friends and could have set aside this situation quite easily without harming anyone. The Father of the Stumpf sons came and burned down a farm and a windmill, but without ever writing us in advance about his anger.[90] I would have preferred to go after my other enemies, especially the ones from Cologne, the bishop of Bamberg, and others who were the root of my misfortune, but this ruthless man prevented this. I now had to also defend myself against them because I was notified that the old Stumpf was recruiting men. To find out more information about this, I started scouting near Thomeneck. Five riders arrived who wanted to meet the old Stumpf. I threw all five to the ground and one of them died. When we ambushed them, the five of them were together in the Hardthäuser Forest, but one of them split off. If I had noticed this, then I could have surely captured him too.

About the men from Cologne: The Master of Hanau took control of the prisoners and said they were under his protection because one man from Hanau was among them. But the von Huttens claimed they were under their protection, so therefore I had to get involved and was fighting five feuds at once. If I could have rallied my men quick enough, Sir Frowin von Hutten[91] would have been my prisoner. I would have captured

---

[90] A letter had to be written in advance announcing the beginning of a feud.
[91] Frowin von Hutten was part of one the oldest Frankish noble families. He was also a regular advisor to the Kaiser himself, and later a patron of his relative, prominent Reformist intellectual Ulrich von Hutten.

him not only because he was resentful about his prisoner, but also because he sent threats against me. I learned that the Bishop of Mainz, whose Hofmeister[92] he was, had sent him towards Erfurt. I therefore took one of my bravest knights, who I liked very much, and rode in the same direction. When we arrived at the area, we stayed with a friend and asked around about when Sir von Hutten would leave. My plan was to follow him after he left and then capture him before he arrived in Sallmünster. But I could not find my knights at the place I ordered them to go, and therefore my plan was ruined once again. When I learned of his arrival in Sallmünster, I still remained around the area for two or three more days, but because this was his home, it was impossible to find out when he would leave from there. I could not remain in this region for much longer and had to bitterly retreat. The old man von Hutten was a good friend of mine who I did not seriously want antagonize anyway, because he was an honorable and just man. If I would have confronted him, then all I would have done was to simply ask him a question on what he plans to do. If he was determined in his plan then I would take him on his knight's honor and fight him appropriately, but if he was friendly and did not mean it in a serious way, then I would have taken his side and released him. This was my intent from the start, but as mentioned, the situation ended differently.

---

[92] Similar to a Privy Counsellor, a high-ranking personage in a princely court.

Part IX

I still had business with the bishop of Bamberg that happened like this: My relative Eustachius von Thüngen became the bishop's enemy and captured two boats on the River Main which were owned by the city of Frankfurt. During this time, I was riding along the Westerwald [93] towards Franconia and did not know of my relative's troubles because I had to defend my own business in my feud against Cologne. I arrived very tired at a Thüngian castle because I had not gotten a good night of sleep for sixteen days. When I asked my relative who all these knights and riders were, he admitted that he planned to attack the bishop of Bamberg. I had already had problems with the bishop of Bamberg twice before. Therefore, I did not care about my exhaustion and marched with my relative at night. When we met up with his riders, he got a message. I noticed that he wanted to retreat because some Würzburgian riders were arriving by ship. I gave him the advice that he could do whatever he wants. He should be aware, though, that this plan would not stay secret, because there were many riders and footmen with us from many different places who would not remain silent. He would have also had no chance to repeat this attack for many years. I said that if he wanted to hear my opinion, then we should not retreat but instead try our luck. We would still be strong enough, even if the Würzburgian knights arrived. He also did not have a feud with the bishop of Würzburg, and the roads were not in his region or rule. My relative followed my advice without disagreement. I led the men forward when I felt it was the right time, and the others followed slowly. I climbed up a mountain near the Main along a trail, and scouted for the

---

[93] The "Western Forest," a heavily wooded region on the Middle Rhine.

ships. There were many sharpshooters on the mountain who I thought were on our side. I yelled over that now was the time to begin. When I rode along the mountain, I found many wine gardens. I saw a path that led all the way to the Main. There were two old loyal footmen guarding the exit. They were Rieneckers[94] and without a doubt just and honorable men. They had bolts on their crossbows, and even though I only had one young man with me, I still spoke and said: "Who are you?" They responded that they were Rieneckers and had four handgunners on foot with them. I told them to be at ease, and one of them asked me who we were. I told him we were Thüngian. He shouted: "Oh! You will doom my lord today." I responded that we were not planning anything evil against his lord, and that he should remain calm and peaceful. Götz von Thüngen and Georg von Gebsattel waited there for a while with their men until Eustachius von Thüngen had also arrived. I told him he should take the two old footmen under his protection, but that he had to ensure that they would not raise the alarm or warn more men. He did so, and I reminded him again that now was time to act. He led us through an old fort, across the Main, which mostly disused. This made me happy because he proved himself to be a thoughtful rider. When we crossed the river, I said to Götz von Thüngen and Georg von Gebsattel: "Stay with the riders, because if we fire at them and they fire back at us from the ship, then this will be our loss and their advantage. I'm going to ride to them and talk to them." I rode as close as possible to the ship and yelled: "Those Würzburgians and Rieneckers who value their life should leave the boat, and we shall have no troubles with them." One yelled back and asked if they will be safe. I responded that everything and everyone that is Rieneckian or Würzburgian would remain untouched, but that we would treat the Bambergers like they deserved. They instantly loaded up a small boat, similar to the ones most big ships have attached them, with so many footmen

---

[94] i.e., men from the small County of Rieneck.

that I swear I was worried it would sink. Like this not a single shot was fired from our or their side. If one party had started firing, I cannot tell how this situation would have ended or if our plan would have been successful. If I myself had been in such a ship with so many footmen, then I would not have been afraid, even with a thousand riders outside. This is why I believe that my relative Eustachius would not have succeeded that day without me or without the grace of God. We let the horses drag the small boat and the ship to land, and filled up sixteen wagons with various valuables, but only took what was Bambergian, and hauled the entire loot in the same night towards Reisenberg.

I want to now explain shortly how the situation with the Bishop of Bamberg at Heidelberg occurred. When my dearest Kurfürst and lord, the Pfalzgraf Ludwig, celebrated his marriage with the sister of Herzog Wilhelm of Bavaria, many young men of nobility rode to the celebrations as is tradition. We all wore the same clothes, nothing expensive, but we were well respected and we received more honors than we deserved. We even were seated together in a place of honor. It then occurred like this: My brother-in-law Martin von Sickingen and I walked up the stairs into the Hirsch inn. My brother-in-law walked ahead. When we reached the top, we saw the bishop of Bamberg leaning on a nearby railing, who gave my brother-in-law a handshake. He then also gave me his hand. After we shook hands, I walked over to Graf Ludwig of Hanau, who was a pious young man, and told him: "The bishop just gave me a handshake. I do not think he knew who I was. He did not recognize me or else he would have not given it to me." The bishop heard this because I spoke loudly, and came towards me and said that he gave me his hand but did not know who I was. I responded: "Sir, you did not know me, and I hereby take the handshake back." This is when a maiden near me walked away and into the rooms of Pfalzgraf Ludwig and Bishop Lorenz of Würzburg, both of whom I liked. The bishop of Bamberg got so angry that his face turned red like a crab because he had shaken my hand. He must have known that I helped my relative Eustachius von Thüngen when he raided the ships on the Main. I myself had two troubles with him prior, but those were put to rest.

I do not want to lie to anybody, and admit that I knowingly became the enemy of Nuremburg and dealt with that trouble accordingly. I first thought to myself that I had to start trouble with the foolish bishop of Bamberg so that the Nurembergers would get dragged into it. I captured around ninety-five merchants who were travelling for the bishop, but I was honorable enough to only take what was Nurembergian. Thirty of those I captured on the Monday after the day of our Lord's Ascension,[95] between eight and nine, and then rode with them the following night and Wednesday. I kept the good Hans von Selbitz always by my side, with about thirty riders besides. My companion Hans von Selbitz also became the bishop's enemy a fortnight later and burned down a castle and a town which was, if I remember correctly, named Filseck.

Around the same time the Reichstag of Trier began, but the location was moved to Cologne.[96] I therefore hid my prisoners somewhere safe and made my way towards the River Rhine to scout out the roads towards Cologne. I remained with a close friend for a while and acted along his advice. My plan was to capture the Nurembergian and Bambergian advisors when they came riding up the Rhine. I was informed, though, that the Nurembergians were arriving by ship, and not by horses. I remained near Bacharach at an inn, as I wanted to eat breakfast and had none of my troops with me, only some acquaintances. One of them wore Pfalzgrafian colors and planned to leave soon. One man came in saying that a merchant was waiting outside next to the Rhine. He was Bambergian and wanted to ask his master for an armed guard so he could travel safely. The boy was nobility and from the

---

[95] Forty days after Easter.
[96] This was the Reichstag of 1512.

Seckendorfer family. Sadly, neither his master nor his servants were at home. One citizen walked out to him and told him that the roads were safe and that there was enough protection on the Rhine anyway that he did not need any more. The boy disagreed and said he did not want to move without protection. I then climbed onto the city gate, near where the vineyards with their high hills were. I gave an order to pay close to attention to this situation, and said that in an emergency they knew where to find me. The bishop left the ship and entered with his entire entourage into the inn where I was also staying. There was nobody in there who could have offered them protection besides the one man with Pfalzgrafian colors, who was only there because of me. He had no alternative and had to offer them protection, due to the obligations of a nobleman's code of honor.

Part X

So that everyone finally understands how I got into conflict and feud with the Nurembergers, I shall now explain how it happened. Fritz von Littwach, a Markgrafian servant with whom I was raised as a squire and as a knight, had done a lot of good deeds for me but disappeared suddenly near Ansbach. He was kidnapped and taken prisoner, and nobody even knew what happened to him for a long time. It took a long time until the Markgraf captured someone who supposedly aided in kidnapping him. It was only through this man that we even found out that he was captured and who captured him. Hans von Seckendorf, the Markgrafian Hofmeister of the time, was close friends with Fritz von Littwach and was very upset about how his friend was treated so dishonorably. I therefore asked him, as my relative who had done me many good deeds, to get me the Urfehde[97] of the traitor who caused all this. He agreed to do so, and it became obvious that Nurembergian servants caused all of this. We therefore knew that he was held in their residences and castles.

This was the root of my feud with the Nurembergians, because Fritz von Littwach was a man of good spirits and always ready to aid me.

To add onto this: I once had a squire named Georg von Geißlingen, who offered his services to me. The Nurembergers, with the posse of Eustachius von Liechtenstein, wounded him so brutally that he died. His master was also harmed, but he survived. Even though we had many reasons for our hostility, we still did not know where Fritz von Littwach was. I saw nobody who tried to, as they say, put the chains on the cat.[98]

---

[97] The document officially renouncing a feud.
[98] i.e., to take matters into their own hands.

Only the poor, loyal, and charitable Götz von Berlichingen took on both of these injustices. These reasons are the ones I always kept stating over and over again to the Nurembergers, in front of Imperial commissioners, and in front of princes both temporal and ecclesiastical. Now I want to further describe how the Nurembergian feud went for me and my relatives. *In summa summarum*:[99] The Reich brought four hundred riders, among them counts, knights, and servants, against me, and if those Letters of Feud still exist, Acht and Aberacht[100] was declared against me. The monks and priests threw torches at me[101] and would have allowed the birds to eat my body off the streets.[102] Everything I owned was taken from me. In the end I did not have even a spare pair of shoes left. I could not just wallow in this situation but had to act. I captured so much of value from my enemies that the Kaiser repeatedly told his advisors to finally organize a peace settlement between us. Through the delays of the Kaiser, I lost almost 200,000 gulden, and all my motivation to fight against the Nurembergers started to fade. Despite the orders of the Kaiser, no settlement was reached. I would have beaten every single Nurembergian warrior. Even the mayor with his golden chain and iron mace, along with all his guards, even with an entire cohort of mercenaries. With God's mercy I would have beaten and captured every single one of them. I was prepared with riders and footmen. I had my armor ready and it was certain that I

---

[99] Latin for "in summary"

[100] The *Reichsacht* or "Penalty of Eight" was a form of outlawry legally enshrined in Imperial law. For certain crimes—such as refusal to abide by a decision of an Imperial court—offenders could be effectively ostracized, and were legally allowed and encouraged to be killed by any member of the public. This rather extreme form of community enforcement comes from the relative weakness of centralized authority, which often lacked the ability to enforce the law on its own.

[101] A symbolic gesture of excommunication from the Catholic Church.

[102] Those under the *Reichsacht* were often called *Vogelfrei* or "bird-free" because their bodies were to be left unburied, and thus would be eaten by scavenger birds and other wild animals.

was able to achieve victory. But in the end, I had many good friends and nobles whose advice I requested, asking them if I should either begin my plan or try to set up a meeting with the Kaiser. They advised me to honor and appeal to the Kaiser by visiting him. Even with the heavy cost this caused me, I still followed their advice, because if I had followed my plan the situation would still not be settled at the end.

The Kaiser set up another meeting by the next summer between me and the Nurembergers. He ordered his advisors to Würzburg. This is when I came up with a clever plan again. The plan was good and certain this time, because I had many good friends who were all loyal to me and said they would support me. I wanted a charitable Kaiser, good masters, and friends in Franconia, and therefore had to show good will and settle in Würzburg. I had to hand off my money so the entire situation did not drag on any further.

After this settlement with the Kaiser, I was still enemies with the Nurembergers and planned a very profitable ambush with my friends against them. I wanted to capture their merchants on their way to Franconia between Nuremberg and Fürth along with their guards. I showed this plan only to my friends and the captain I had with me, who was also a close friend of mine. I believed that they would have no bad thoughts about this plan, and that they were ready to claim honor and loot, so that after this we could finally achieve a fair and adequate settlement. This plan was sadly not meant to be. Many of them acted like they already were locked in the city's towers by just seeing the enemy, and I had to accept the settlement as it was. I always fought my battles so that they would end quickly. Through God's grace and help I always achieved a fair and quick peace. I cannot think of a single feud or hostility that lasted longer than two years, which wasn't long for such troubles. Once, a ruler[103] informed me through his own captains and my brother that I would die as his enemy,

---

[103] This was very likely the Kurfürst of Mainz.

but through the power of our Almighty God, it became the shortest feud I ever had. It is also true that it was my intent, as the enemy of the Nurembergians, to capture a large merchant convoy they led. My scout, who did not follow my orders correctly, ruined this plan in a matter of thirty minutes and I attacked the wrong wagon. The merchants, who thought I had attacked the wagon on purpose because of its valuable cargo, ran to Kaiser Maximilian, who was in Augsburg at the time, fell to their knees and held speeches about how evil I was. They claimed their lives were ruined, that the damages were so bad that they could never recover. The good Kaiser gave them this response: "Dear God! Holy God! What is this? One of them only has one hand, the other only one leg. What would you merchants do if they had both hands and both legs!" This was said about me and Hans of Selbitz. The Kaiser supposedly also said:

"What's going on here? If a merchant loses a bag of pepper the entire Reich should be alarmed and send troops, but when Imperial Royalty is in need of trade that concerns lords, dukes, other kingdoms and the entire Reich, then the merchants are nowhere to be found!" I heard of this speech around three or four days after it occurred from a nobleman who heard of it himself by a letter from Augsburg. I liked this speech of my Kaiser so much that it filled my heart with joy. I cannot remember that I ever did anything in my life against the Kaiser or the House of Austria. I could have easily gone to the place where crowns are worn and much gold flows,[104] but did not do so out of respect for the Kaiser, and rather aided him as a knight and rider and survived many dangers for him that not many would survive.

I still did not mention one event. I found out, still as an enemy of Nuremberg, that many wagons with goods travelled through the forest named Hagenschieß. I was travelling with

---

[104] Suggesting that he could have carried out a lucrative business committing robberies in the rich lands of the Austrian Habsburgs.

my master and many other good comrades during this time. We had endured many troubles together already. This was when I got the news of the wagons arriving. We marched out and attacked them, but they showed us that they were under Pfalzgrafian protection. I never heard that Pfalzgrafian protection was valid in this area, but thought that only Imperial protection was allowed. [105] My scout told me specifically how these matters were around here. I later learned that my scout had a big mouth. An innkeeper had informed the merchants of our plans, and they got the correct protection. I let them go in the end, because I was on good terms with the Pfalzgrafians. The Pfalz was always close to my heart for many reasons, which is why I always spared those with the graces of the Kurfürst.

When those wagons moved on, I got the idea for another ambush. I knew that when the Frankfurt Fair began, that the Nurembergers would travel on foot out of Würzburg towards Frankfurt and through Lengefeld towards the Spessart. After I sent out scouts to confirm this, I captured five or six of them with one merchant among them. I had captured this merchant for the third time in half a year, and once even taken his goods. The others were basket weavers from Nuremberg. I got up and stood over them as if I planned to cut all their hands and arms off, but I was not being serious. They had to kneel and put their hands on blocks, but then I only kicked their behinds and gave the other a slap across the ear. This was all the punishment I had for them, and I let them go. The merchant who I captured multiple times was astounded by what happened and said: "I would have rather expected for the sky to collapse than to be captured again by you. I heard at the market in Nuremberg that you just captured some wagons in the Hagenschieß a couple of nights ago. I am therefore quite surprised that you got here so quickly." I was surprised myself about how quickly alerts about my travels could arrive in Nuremberg.

---

[105] The right to control traffic on the roads was often a subject of feudal right.

The Kaiser got involved after this and settled the feud in Würzburg, like I earlier mentioned. I described this event to show every knight and honorable man that the ones from Nuremburg put a lot of effort into this and even spied on their enemies. The "Poor Kunz"[106] began as soon as I settled my matters with Nuremberg in Würzburg. I instantly rode to the Herzog and he, my brother, and I got thirty horses together as quick as we could. I almost got into trouble there. The Hofmeister Philipp von Nippenburg was our captain of cavalry, and my brother-in-law Jacob von Bernhausen, who at the time was the governor of Waiblingen, travelled with him. This man once met me at the gates of Waiblingen and told me: "Brother-in-law Götz, one man is currently leaving the gates. Do your best to capture him, for he is a troublemaker." I rushed towards my residence and only grabbed two riding spurs, my sword, and my servant, and went after him. We tried to find him, but the vineyards he escaped into had thick bushes, as was normal for the time of the year. We could not see if he was hiding in there or where else he could have run off to. We could not have seen or heard anyone there, fugitive or not. We went towards a valley and noticed a cohort in battle formation going up a steep mountain, the Kappelberg. We spectated them for quite a while, and while we were sitting on our behinds paying no attention to our surroundings, three Weidlians, with full armor down to their knees, one with a gun, one with a halberd, and the third with a long spear, appeared next to us. They spoke and asked what we were doing here. I said: "What would we be doing here? We are taking a walk!" One good looking Weidlian man, who was a bit advanced in age, responded: "Do we also want to take a walk?"[107] I disagreed with him and said, "You

---

[106] This was a peasant revolt started by a farmer named Kunz or Conrad in the year 1514. It aimed to remove Herzog Ulrich of Württemberg from power and raided many monasteries and castles. The peasants supposedly carried with them a dead farmer in a coffin who had the words "The Poor Kunz" written on his forehead.

[107] At the risk of pointing out the obvious, these are "fighting words."

see that we are not prepared for a fight." He responded, "We would rather fight you when you are prepared for it." "Well then," I said, "I hear and see that you are a warrior. Let us quickly get armed and come back with exactly the three men you see before you right now." Both parties agreed to this arrangement. We hurried back home to arm ourselves but when we came near the city, we saw eight hundred men from Tübingen coming towards it, intending to swear their loyalty to the Herzog of Württemberg. I was worried they would arrive at the gate before us. We started running as quick as we could towards the gate and hurried up getting our armor on. We left the city so quickly again that not even my own brother knew what we were up to. All well and done, we arrived back at where we met those three good men, but they were nowhere to be found. We searched up and down, but they had simply disappeared. While we waited, the leader of the peasant revolt marched towards the city and came to our captain with some of his scoundrels. I said, "This is the captain Hans Wagenbach from Schorndorf, I know him." We attempted to ride to him to tell him of our scouting experience, and when we arrived, I said: "Wagenbach, you have three men under your command, I do not know their names. Those three challenged us to a fight and we left to get armed, but when we came back, they were gone. Try to find them, and tell them that we came to you to make clear that we kept our promise but they did not." He got very angry about those men and said he would punish them. I disagreed and told him, "No, no, do not harm them. Just tell them that we kept our promise but could not find them. If we would have found each other, then all we would have done is strangle each other and the matter would have been settled anyway." A long time after the revolt was defeated, I met my brother-in-law Jacob von Bernhausen, but I do not remember if it was in Stuttgart or somewhere else. He told me: "Brother-in-law Götz, I heard of a man who wants to offer his services to you and said he would follow you for a hundred miles." My brother-in-law also added that he was the best warrior in all of

Württemberg. The man was from Winterbach, which was close to Waiblingen, but I cannot remember the specifics, I even forget his name. I liked him and told my brother-in-law the more the merrier. I learned through his reputation that he would be a good fighter. In the end, it was good that we could not find each other that day because we would have all strangled each other for no good cause or reason.

The earlier mentioned captain, Hans Wagenbach, remained with the Herzog and served him well. He was chased away and held out with him until the Herzog could return to his lands. Certainly not all men stuck to their colors like this. I rejected my war service before the Herzog marched on Reutlingen because I did not know if he had been declared an enemy of the League.[108] If this matter would have been settled quicker, then I would have not rejected my service and would have served for the Kaiser. I had already agreed to follow my brother-in-law Franz von Sickingen. I therefore left the service half a year early to ride home but I swore to myself to not fight against the Herzog of Württemberg or against the Pfalz again. He promised me this too and said this shall never happen. But the Herzog then came to Reutlingen and captured it. This is when my chain of bad luck began. This caused more trouble than anything else in my life. Kaiser Maximilian also died shortly after the siege of Reutlingen. After I was captured near Möckmühl, I was then jailed for three and a half years by the League in Heilbronn. My dear God still kept me alive through all of this and I persevered. The League captured all of Württemberg, every fort, castle, city, and house besides the city of Asperg, which survived only a couple of days longer. The League marched down with the intent to overrun us and catch me in a mousetrap near Möckmühl. The cats were already waiting behind the traps to eat the mouse. That is how it happened that I was captured. At first, they held onto three

---

[108] The aforementioned Swabian League, the major political power in South Germany at the time.

places—Weinsberg, Neuenstadt and Möckmüh—with whom I honorably discussed terms. I cannot remember if this lasted two or three weeks because I had so many agreements, settlements and disputes around this time that I cannot remember many of them. I have to say that I could have held out longer in the mousetrap near Möckmühl, but the three forts Weinsberg, Neuenstadt and Möckmühl turned their back on the Herzog, joined the Alliance, and broke their promise to me and the Herzog, as people who only sit behind and do nothing often will.

I now want to shortly describe how I was being treated back then: The League marched into Möckmühl because the city itself was also opposed to me, and demanded that they turn over the house and the fort in which I resided. They argued for a long time about this, specifically Hans von Ehrenberg, Florian Geyer,[109] one cannon master, and many others whose names I cannot remember. The cannon master spoke first and said: "If he does not want to surrender the castle, then give him more than just nice words." We then signed a contract which guaranteed my men and I free leave with our life, possessions, horses and even our weapons and armor. They had already carried the cannons up to the church, which was named Dechanei and adjoined up to the castle near the gate. My relatives and I were satisfied with this contract. We only had three bags of flour left in the entire place and the citizens of the city took their crates and barrels inside, so that we could not grab any food. We also had a couple of sheep, which I stole from the citizens and herded up to the castle in front of their eyes. We were also out of shot. I only had some scrap and tin that I broke off from the windows and doors so that I was prepared if they tried to storm us. We did not even have water for the horses. My wine was all that was left, and we had to share it with the horses. Corn and yeast were also very scarce, and we

---

[109] The famous German peasant revolt leader and knight whose renown would rival Götz himself later in his life.

only had what little I had on myself. The citizens emptied the storage halls, and we would have had to leave because of hunger alone. This is why I agreed to the contract. I very likely could have survived this situation unharmed because I had helped the friends of the Herzog before this, specifically Wolf Endriß von Weiler and many others of the nobility who all made it to the castle unharmed. I could have probably taken the same path unnoticed and without harm. I trusted the contract though, and believed they would let me go. This did not happen. I was thrown down, almost killed, and my comrades were strangled and stabbed. Even more so: some troops of the League, who I had met on the battlefield before, told me in secret that the highest captain of the League gave the order to take my life. I could write about more things like this, but I do not think this is necessary. God did not only watch over me in this situation alone, but it seems to me that He watched over me many times during my dangers, troubles and feuds against the many different classes I made enemies of. He gave me his grace, charity, and aid, and cared more for me than I could have myself. It is also true that I was put in an unfortunate, damaging, and disadvantageous position through the injustice done against me.

After this imprisonment I was stuck in a residence near Heilbronn. This was when the League sent a Swiss man from Konstanz to me. He was a scribe of some sort and had an Urfehde with him, which he read aloud with many people listening and demanded that I accept it. If I did not accept it then I would be thrown into the tower as the League demanded. I quickly rejected the Urfehde and said I would rather spend a year in the tower than accept it. I made clear that if I was in an honorable feud and if they treated me as an honorable knight and nobleman is supposed to be treated, then I would have behaved differently. At the time I was in a place that was honorable for an arrested knight, and I hoped they would not take me someplace worse. If I had behaved in an unruly manner then they could have taken me to such a place.

I could have not behaved myself better though, depriving them of an excuse to do this. They allowed me to visit the church and go back to my residence on my own. When I stepped out of the church and wanted to speak with someone, I had to take them to the residence and could not speak to them on the street. I did so to not look suspicious. In short: Because I did not sign the Urfehde, they ordered the Weinschröters[110] to me. They then stormed into my room in the Ditz residence and tried to arrest me again. I instantly grabbed my sword and they stood back. The citizens from the city council asked me to let go of my sword, and said that they only wanted to talk to me in the city hall. Right when they took me there, my wife[111] came up the steps because she had just gone to church. I ripped myself away from them and ran to her and said: "My wife, do not be scared. They force an Urfehde against me. I do not want to sign it and would rather let myself be thrown in the tower. Ride away to Franz von Sickingen and Sir Georg von Frundsberg and tell them that they do not want to treat me with knight's honor anymore. They will know, as noble knights, how to respond to this!" My wife did so. The men of the League took me to the city hall and from there into the tower, in which I had to spend the night. On Pentecost evening they did the same, and the next morning they took me out towards the city hall again. Many advisors were in the main hall with me. My wife, who had come back from the camp, stood before the door. They supposedly heard that the entire cohort was marching against the city again on both foot and horseback. This is when I whispered my plan into my wife's ear: "Tell my brother-in-law Franz von Sickingen and Georg von Frundsberg to discuss terms, for my sake, but also tell them, if they have a plan, to only act on it if I was stabbed and killed." She successfully delivered this message. Sir Georg and many others came to the city hall and

---

[110] A term of unclear meaning, literally an occupational name for a maker of wine barrels, but more probably a family name, referring to some family involved in the intrigue against Götz.
[111] Dorothea of Saxonheim

argued on my behalf that I shall be jailed in a knightly honor for as long as the war lasted and until the League reached a peace. This settlement is still in my possession until this day. When the League released me, I had to pay them 2000 gulden in gold, which was received by the men who had captured me. Even though I did not own much, I still gathered enough together through my good friends and master. I sent the money to Ulm and they supposedly had a good time with it.

Further, when my brother-in-law Franz von Sickingen became an enemy of Worms, me and many other friends organized seventy or eighty horses for him on our own behalf even though he wanted to pay us. We did not accept any of it but instead wanted to serve him for free, because he would do the same for us. I became an enemy of the Erzstift[112] of Mainz one month later and Thomas von Rosenberg wanted to avenge Boxberg,[113] which we accomplished. It was in the year of 1515, near my wedding date, when we became enemies of Mainz. The next spring in the year 1516 I captured the old Graf Philipp of Waldeck,[114] with whom I achieved a settlement quite quickly and through him settled the general feud. The bishop said, like earlier mentioned in the feud with Mainz, that I would die as his enemy; despite this the feud was settled rather quickly. Dearest God made this feud the shortest of all, luckily without anyone ruining my plans through their foolishness, as with the multiple incidents I described earlier.

Soon after this, Franz von Sickingen marched against the Herzog of Lothringia and took a castle of his, which was called Schaumberg. It soon came to a settlement and Franz marched back. Fritz von Thüngen and I sent all our horses and troops which we could gather to Franz. I would have participated

---

[112] An Erzstift was a territory ruled by the Church. In the case of Mainz it was also a Kurfürstum, one of the seven Imperial Electors. This made it a rather formidable enemy for Götz.

[113] Rosenberg's castle near the Odenwald, which was burned down by his enemies.

[114] Graf Philipp's ransom is recorded at 8,900 ducats, a massive sum.

myself, but while the Grafs Albrecht of Mansfeld and Philipp of Solms tried to solve the matter between myself and Mainz, I had to wait. All this happened in the years 1515 and 1516.

Part XI

Now I want to tell the story of how I came into conflict and feud with the Stift of Mainz. It happened like this: I rode out of the city to Grünfeld after I reached a settlement with the Nurembergers. A noble lived there with the name Bartholomäus Hund, who owned the residence himself. He asked me if I was unaware of how my own farmers are doing in my hometown. I said no, because I truly did not know. He told me some men from Buchen destroyed a large farmland of ten to twelve morgen.[115] The farms are in a place called Lappen and are separated by a hedge which is also called the Lappen. it was almost ripe for farming, if the ones from Buchen had not led their animals purposefully and dishonorably through the field. They claimed the land was theirs and that the farmers of my hometown had no right to cultivate it. This was wrong; to this day these fields belong to me and to my descendants. I responded to Bartholomäus Hund: "It seems like I am going from one war to the next. I only made peace with Nuremberg yesterday and now some other troubles are already stirring up." I instantly rode to Jagsthausen and met a man who came from Hainstadt. His name was Christmann, a truly pious man. I asked him what occurred and how things were. I had heard damage was done to them. He then described to me everything that occurred just as it was described to me earlier, and even more. After I heard this, I quickly wrote to the Bucheners that they should pay compensation to my poor people for those unjust, dishonorable and violent actions. But they did not care. I was writing letters back and forth with the Bucheners and the Bishop of Mainz for a year. The bishop set up multiple

---

[115] A morgen was a square unit of land measurement during the time. The size of a morgen varied from 1/2 to 2 1/2 acres (2,000 to 10,100 square meters).

meetings, which I attended, but the ones from Buchen did not. He then set up a meeting in Bischofsheim which I also visited. The officials of Mainz were there, Leonhard von Thurn and Wolf von Hartheim. They were supposed to hear our issues but instead played chess. This insulted me greatly. They also had disagreements with each other and beat each other severely. I was also told that they spoke about not giving anything to Nuremberg. I myself did not think that idea was all that bad. To sum it up quickly: We did not reach a conclusion. I now knew what I had to do. I wrote the Bishop of Mainz a feud letter and let him stew in it. I gathered my resources and started planning an ambush. The scouts reported back about the state of things in the Mainz area, and we made a plan to capture the Bishop in Aschaffenburg near the Hofzaun while he was under Frankfurtian protection. I took this matter seriously. I gathered one hundred to one hundred and fifty horses, and was certain to harm the bishop and his trades with this because I knew he would be in a hurry. My troops halted near the upper Hofzaun so they could occupy the area, and thirty-two horses and myself rode day and night until we arrived in the Dammfeld, where I was ready to attack them. Even though I received reports about the roads from Nuremberg until Frankfurt, I wanted to make absolutely sure, and sent one of my men to Wildenberg. He was supposed to see how strong they were and what routes they took. On the day of my wife's birthday, at a resting spot near Dammfelde, he would, if God's grace allowed it, meet us and report back. Whoever arrived first would wait for the others. I met him at the spot we discussed and asked him how the things were and in what strength they marched towards Miltenberg. He reported that eight had marched in, and he did not see any more. He did not watch them for long though, because the entire cohort would have noticed him. This would have scared off some of them because the richest merchants of the Reich were with them, carrying around four to five tons of gold that we could capture. I was scared of messing up if I let those merchants get away, but I could not move away from our positions because such a huge group as mine would surely be noticed. I told myself it is better to only get a bit than nothing at all, and that with eight thousand gulden the war would still start off in a good way, but my main plan was ruined. I captured the ones my scout mentioned and the feud began. If I did not leave to meet up with my riders right as the night struck then I would have captured everyone, even the ones on the Spessart, but this was not meant to be and everyone returned to their homes.

I now told my men that the Bucheners started this war and are therefore just and honorable targets to attack. They did so as well as they could because they were only five or six horses strong. The rest I left to God's mercy, and retreated back to a safe place to give the horses some rest. I released my men to one place or another so I had nobody with me besides my boy, who told me that my horse was doing badly because it had gotten no new shoes for a while. This reminded me of a good smith I knew in Marbach. I then rode to him to get new shoes on my horse. I came to an innkeeper, whose name was Schreiber, and who I knew. There I thought to eat a bit myself while my horse was being cared for. That's when he told me that the Mainzers stayed there last night on their way home with sixteen horses and twelve wagons. He also told me that a council was called by the League, but that he did not know where. I assumed it would be in Ulm at the Bundestag. I told my boy to get my horse ready as quick as he could. We then ate a bit and sat on the horses. I did not even allow myself the time to notify or give orders to my men. We arrived at Türkheim, where I knew a path which led behind the Pferch near Eßlingem above the Filz. I had ridden there alone in day time, but at night I thought I would miss the path and therefore hired a peasant from the area who led me there at nighttime. After this I released him again. When it became really dark, I had to feel the road with my spear because there are ditches and stones, as anyone knows who traveled the road between Göppingen and Eßlingen. When I fell into a ditch, I could not see how I could get out, so I had to help myself as best as I could. Finally, I arrived at my comrade's place and took six men with me and rode on. Finally, I accomplished my task and I captured the Bundesrat on the road towards Ulm. I avoided all Württembergian roads. My task and search were finally a success on St. Lucia's Day[116] in the year of 1515. The League Council came with six guards, and among them was the Kaiser's personal gunsmith. I did not harm him in any way, and even gave him friendly greetings. I told my riders that when everything was safe, they should only steal from his companions and not let anyone escape, because I wanted to talk with the master on my own. Everyone among them behaved well. The council had their squires with them. One of them recognized me and said: "It truly is the one and only Götz!" I was already throwing them on the ground, but he offered to surrender without any trouble. I appreciated this gesture, but it was truly not part of my plan. Staying in that area for a while would have been disadvantageous, as it was not safe. I tried to seize him but his head hit against my equipment and twisted my sword. The sword gave him quite a gash, which bled heavily. I got very scared for him and quickly gave him a Blutwurzel[117] to stop the bleeding, which luckily did the trick. I carried the prisoners off to a place I considered safe, and patted myself on the back about how well all this went. Sadly, my hiding spot was revealed by a person with a big mouth, and my prisoners were stolen from me by a nobleman from the House of Württemberg. People say that Max Strumpf gained his current title through this exploit, but in my opinion, this seems rather unlikely because he already possessed the title by this time. I told the person who was taking care of my prisoners to inform me if he was not able to hold onto them

---

[116] December 13th

[117] A *blutwurzel* is a root of the tormentil plant (*Potentilla erecta*), which was used as an anti-inflammatory medicine in premodern times. It's unclear if Götz intends this meaning, which would be unlikely to treat a slash wound, or if he means some other sort of herbal poultice or bandage.

anymore, because I already had another spot in mind. I also told him to treat the one prisoner with the respect he deserved. The entire plan was not built around this one person though, so I also had to make sure the others were treated appropriately. My servant told me that I should not be afraid, and that if something dangerous happened he knew how to treat them and to bring them to a better place.

I was now in the mood to make the area unsafe for a while and to keep trying my luck. Revenge motivated me during this, and therefore, with not more than seven men, I burned down three places, Ballenberg, Oberndorf, and the sheep house close to Krautheim below the Schloßberg. I have to admit that I usually did not enjoy wrecking and burning down places, but this time I wanted to do it so that the overseer of the region would finally reveal himself. To give him time to respond, I waited an hour or two at a place between Krautheim and Neuenstadt on a snow-bright night. The official started screaming at me while we set the walls aflame, but I told him to lick my behind.[118] This was not a time to rest and I had to quickly move on. On the third day of my attacks, I captured a man from Miltenberg whose name was Reußlein. He carried three sets of fine silverware with him. After this I directed my travels towards a more distant land. The reason for this was that six canons and councilors were on their way to Halle,[119] in Saxony, to call upon the Archbishop of Mainz with fourteen other companions. From what I knew, they were very rich men. I sent out the best scouts I had and heard that they were already on their way back, but all this dragged on for so long that I lost an entire month of preparation time. I occupied three places at this point: the Thuringian Forest, Franconia, and

---

[118] This toned-down version corresponds to the more *en vogue* South German saying, "Lick my ass." It is assumed that he actually said something more akin to this, and Goethe also used the latter wording to characterize his rather honest and direct mannerisms.

[119] The Kurfürst of Mainz was also the Archbishop of Magdeburg at the same time. His residence was in Halle, and his name was Albrecht von Brandenburg.

Buchen. No matter which street they took, they would fall into my hands. My troops were in Hesse at the time, and I ordered them to occupy the paths there but to not do anything, no matter what happened, and to wait for my orders. We would have certainly had a successful ambush, if they would have followed my plan. They did not listen, and instead raided two villages in the region of Ammelberg, looting them and burning them down; this ruined my plan. When the councilors arrived in Ammelberg, which belonged to the Bishop of Mainz, and heard that these villages were burned down, they went back on the road at night with fresh horses and ran off. I later learned that they carried thirty-four thousand gulden to Frankfurt. This money was given to the Fuggers,[120] who then lent the money to the Pope in Rome for the pallium.[121] Great damages were done to me at this time through the foolishness of my men.

After this I learned that someone had offered me his home to stay around Westphalia. I did not know of this before, but was very happy about the offer, and went on my way to take a look at the place. I arrived in the afternoon of Palm Sunday.[122] I visited Mass on Palm Sunday as any good Christian is supposed to, and the hosts who offered me their home took me aside after Mass and told me that the Graf of Waldeck contacted them. They were supposed to meet with him near a place named Adorf. When they arrived, he informed them that he was very displeased with them taking in an enemy of the Archbishopric. He said he would not hide the fact that he was very fond of the archbishop. They were related, and therefore

---

[120] The Fuggers were a preeminent banking family in Europe, and did a tremendous business with the Habsburg dynasty.
[121] A pallium is a vestment symbolizing the authority of an Archbishop—the implication being that this money was lent essentially as a bribe to secure a candidate's nomination to the seat. Götz gets one detail wrong, though. Fugger lent the money to the Archbishop, who then gave it to the Pope. The Pope was widely unpopular and corruption in the Church a hot-button issue, making the accusation somewhat scandalous.
[122] The Sunday before Easter.

he had an interest in his cities, castles, and the entire region. He was also his advisor, and gave him counsel when needed. I was supposed to stop the burnings, release the prisoners, and return all the goods that were stolen. With this he declared himself an enemy against me. This act was understandable and done honorably. It would have been to my great disadvantage if he did not act so honorably. I would have until this day not known that he was aligned to the archbishop. I would have not worried about him at all and would not have even prepared any defenses. My two friends then asked me what they should do with this situation. "What could my advice be? He declared himself as our enemy so we will treat him as our enemy." They then asked: "What can we do?" I said: "I am unknown here and I do not know anybody in this region, so I could approach both friend and enemy by accident. But if we could send out scouts and gather information, then we could predict his plans and can act against them." They appreciated this advice and sent out scouts, and learned that he stayed in a castle named Wildungen. It was on a high hill right next to a small town. He had a wild spring there where he liked to bathe. I had ridden past it the previous afternoon without knowing the Graf was my enemy. Now I knew he would leave soon towards Jülich, where he was to receive a permanent governorship over Arnsberg. I learned on the day of his leave that the Herzog of Jülich, his sister's son, gave him this title. I thought to myself, why should I hire men around this area, where I may meet either friend or enemy, when I had a good servant with me who I trusted greatly? I asked him if he could not try to hire twelve riders. I told him the places from where I would like them, and he responded: "Oh yes my lord, I know where to go." I asked him where the location was in detail, and he responded: "The house named Hahn, where stays Georgs of Bischoffsrat. He was also the enemy of the Abbott of Fulda and always had ten to fifteen riders with him. He told me that he would aid with troops if you needed them." I yelled out: "Damn it! I captured him once when he was a servant and master of horse for Nuremberg, and we were in a feud. Do you think I can allow myself to ask him?" My servant responded: "That's what he told me." I continued: "Very well. Georg of Bischoffsrat upholds good and honorable friendships and has an honorable father. In his honor I also treated him well back then and let him escape. Go ahead and ride to him. Tell him you informed me of his generous offer and that I am very thankful and would have done the same for him. Please ask him to gather as many men as he can recruit quickly and to send them my way." My servant delivered my message to him, and not long after this the Graf of Waldeck himself arrived in equal numbers to us. I gave two of my men the order to watch the Graf and to follow him, but not to shoot at him or harm him in any way. They only had permission to stab or shoot his horse if he attempted to flee. I myself was interested in fighting his riders. Everything went well and I made quick process with his servants. I then moved on to the Graf. There I found my riders as if they were chained behind him, exactly as I ordered them. I then asked him what I should do with him, after he had taken displeasure with my burnings and declared himself an enemy against me. He responded: "Götz von Berlichingen, is it not better that I was open about my allegiance and did not hide it?" I declared: "Sir, you acted honorably and therefore you shall be treated honorably, but you are still my prisoner." Because he was so honorable, he later paid twenty thousand gulden for the release of himself and his men. I led him and his men away for around thirty minutes through the night. There was a shepherd on the road with his herd, but suddenly five wolves appeared. I found this quite amusing and wished them, like us, good luck. I shouted: "Good luck, dear comrades, luck everywhere you go!" I interpreted this as a good sign and therefore we attacked without much waiting around. I had captured the Graf around Paderborn, so we had to take him first through Colognian territory, through his own region, and then through Hessen towards Hersfeld, which is a

Fürstentum.[123] After this we went through Fulda and Henneberg. From there we went past Saxon, Würzburgian and Bambergian, Margravian, Brandenburgian, Nurembergian, and Pfalzgravian lands. In all there were twelve Fürstentums, plus the city of Nuremberg, through which I took my prisoner until I arrived at our journey's destination. This is when the Bishop of Mainz declared me his foremost enemy until death should take him. The bishop's captain, named Jost, told this to my brother Hans von Berlichingen, who then told it to me. The situation ended differently, and I was not even an enemy of his for more than half a year. They sent someone to me, so that I could agree to a peace settlement, that's how mercifully and graciously God had treated me. Only through God could such a powerful leader desire peace so quickly. This is why nobody should only rely on their title and powers alone. I mentioned this because many liars and resentful people, whoever they may be, like to slander my name because of my troubles with the Graf. I took my enemies in this situation to court and they promised through seals and contract to repay my demands, but they had no honor and did not do so. I can prove this through the handwriting of the Graf of Waldeck and many contract letters. My feud with the bishop, that only lasted half a year, took another half a year of court troubles until a settlement was reached.

    I have to admit that the almighty God gave good luck and grace aplenty to such a poor noble knight as myself. Only because of the foolishness and carelessness of my servants were many of my other great plans ruined, as I have already explained. I participated as a young man in wars, feuds and hostilities, at least fifteen in number, which took a toll on me but which I always fought out until the end. This is all without mentioning all the ones I participated in for the Kaiser, kings, princes, lords, and friends. I have not written down all of them here, but they may be equally as many. Praise God! I do not

---

[123] A Princedom, that is, not subject to any other ruler.

know of a feud that went on for longer than two years without a peace settlement. God the Almighty deserves praise and thanks for this. I am surprised myself that all of these events ended so quickly.

This leads to the previously mentioned troubles. My dear master Graf Albrecht of Mansfeld sent my old riding companion Hans von Selbitz to me and asked me to agree to a meeting between myself and the Prince-Bishop of Mainz, his son, and the Graf of Waldeck. I agreed and the meeting arrived in Schweinfurt. Myself, Graf Albrecht of Mansfeld, and Graf Philipp of Solms, with the Archbishopric of Mainz, agreed to a settlement, and we had a contract and signature in our hands at the end.

Furthermore, it was widely known in this region that Georg von Böttigheim, who was under Kurpfälzian[124] service in his youth, was unjustly thrown off his horse and captured. This was when I, Gottfried von Berlichingen, and my liege at the time, Graf Michael of Wertheim, were approached by the Schenk brothers, Valentin and Eberhard von Erbach. They had just recently entered Pfalzgrafian service, and asked us therefore to avenge the injustice done to Georg von Böttigheim. Because of this I was sent to Heidelberg by the Pfalzgraf, along with the advisors Ludwig Wilhelm von Habern, Graf Michael of Wertheim and the von Erbach brothers. When we arrived, he let us know how to act in the matter concerning Georg von Böttigheim. He supposedly was thrown down for no just reason. The supposed root of all this trouble was Georg von Böttigheim's father. He loaned Konrad Schott[125] one hundred gulden, which he did not pay back over a long period of time. This was given to him in good faith and out of honor, when he still owned land near Hornberg. The Pfalzgraf now was of the opinion that Wilhelm von Habern and I should solve this

---

[124] The Kurpfalz refers to the County Palatine proper, rather than the greater Pfalzgrafian domains of the dynastic branch that ruled it.
[125] The very same troublemaker Konrad "Kunz" Schott mentioned earlier, who was later beheaded by the order of the Markgraf of Ansbach in the year 1524.

trouble as Pfalzgrafian servants. I said to Wilhem von Habern: "Good friend, you know very well that I often asked for help and put many of my friends and lieges in danger and made them worry greatly about me. If one of these friends acted dishonorably then I would have great difficulty raising my hand against them, especially if I did not even announce the feud by letter. If the Pfalzgraf demands us to do our honorable duty as his servants, then we should also uphold our honor to our enemy and announce our feud by letter, or else this dishonor would weigh heavily on our character." This is why we wanted to write the following feud letter explaining the matter:

"Our companion Georg of Böttigheim was unjustly beaten and jailed because he asked for his father's honorably loaned money back. It was said that this loan would be paid back in the form of a horse worth one hundred gulden. When his son came to pick it up and was on his way home to Böttigheim with this horse, he was suddenly thrown down near Möckmühl, captured, and the horse was taken away. It is the common belief therefore that the servants of Konrad Schott did this."

This was not thought without reason. A man was seen with him who declared himself an enemy of the Plfazgraf and who not long after become a servant of his. I saw him once but I forget his name. All I remember is that he was a strong, tall, and portly knight. We declared this letter publicly in many places where we assumed the conspirators were. In these declarations the details of the situation were better described than I have described them here. After this public declaration, both of us, Wilhelm von Habern and I, did our duty to the Pfalzgraf. Soon we received a letter from our beloved Pfalzgraf's council which told us specifically what roads we had to take and how to behave, but I had to throw this letter back at them. I told them I would not ride back through the Hornberg, and asked if they were not aware what dangers I could encounter there. Why were none of the dangers mentioned in the letter? I would have to use my own eyes and see from there what route I would take myself.

I learned myself that Sir Konrad Schott and his companions held a large council with the Markgraf near Ansbach. I therefore planned my attempt there and sent out a scout to a well trusted friend in Ansbach who could gather more detailed information. Right after this, ninety-five horses rode out of the city and stayed in Bergel overnight. I was near Windsheim; during this night I only had fifteen men with me. I knew exactly where the enemy stayed. My plan was therefore as follows: I would let the front of their cohort pass by us and then capture their camp followers while they traveled from Ansbach to Bergel. All of them were armored though, and I had to escape. My arm was struck a few times, how this happened I cannot remember. From Windsheim the path led up a hill until Bergel. One could get up this hill very quickly. I therefore ordered my rider, named Martin Maurer, to move up the hill and to discover if the enemy had already moved on or not. If they came close, he was required to notify me immediately. This rider came to me and said he saw only fifteen men coming in our direction, but I suspected this was only their vanguard. I did not trust him and sent him back up with the order to closely observe what they were doing. I knew they had many horses were around this area, at least ninety-five, and it was a bad path to take for them because only three could ride next to each other at once. This is why he needed to pay close attention to their numbers and to not report me anything false, so we wouldn't burn our hands. He came back and still told me he had only seen fifteen horses. I believed him after this and thought it truly was as he said. I rode close to them until I could see them and, like I suspected, it was only their vanguard. Luckily, I met Hans von Selbitz and my relative Sigmund von Thüngen there, who spoke: "Kinsman, I bid you depart, for not even ten among that cohort are good Pfalzgrafians." But it was too late and my men were already in the midst of battle, beating each other's faces in so heavily that their noses bled. After Sigmund's speech I jumped into the brawl and thundered at them: "What are you doing, Rüsch? Hold back!" As soon as I spoke, they instantly focused on me and started chasing after me, but before they could readjust, I was already ahead of them by a large distance. I escaped with the grace of God and without taking any damage, even though I had many brutish knights hunting me. The true reason for their anger was because they had some dispute with Sigmund von Thüngen. He told them: "See! He is staying still. Go ahead and hunt him down." After this lucky escape I thought I would take the path to Ansbach, with the expectation that I could still meet the men who could aid me with my duty, which did truly come to pass. I met Konrad Schott's wife herself. I left my riders behind me so we would not be spotted, and rode down the path myself to see who actually was in the wagon. As soon as she saw me, she yelled: "Kinsman? Where are you coming from?" I responded "Greetings, sister-in-law, how are you doing? I can barely remember myself where I am coming from." I therefore remained with her until the evening and, after meeting nobody else, I rode to Windsheim. Overnight I had my iron hand repaired because of the damage it had taken earlier.

After this I carried out one or more ambushes in the same region and rested for a couple of days near Frankenberg. Because Konrad Schott remained with my brother-in-law for a while, we captured the Schenk nobleman Friedrich von Limburg in a field. My comrades and I confused him for Konrad Schott because he carried the same weapons and wore the same clothing as him. It was Friedrich von Limburg though, and I reminded him of our Urfehde and released him. Right after this I captured a gunsmith who served Konrad Schott. I took him prisoner and told him to pay a ransom, but I cannot remember if he did or didn't. He was a smart servant who was well liked by Konrad von Schott, and who I also happened to know as a boy. That's how I knew for whom he did his deadly service. I wrote my dear Pfalzgraf that if Konrad Schott wished to free him from certain death, then I would release him in Heidelberg. He remained under arrest in my residence without making any trouble. Treating our enemies in such fashion was not common even for captains and princes. Not long after this I heard of a grand festival that was supposed to take place in in Haßfurt. At this point Konrad von Schott captured and beat a young man who was a relative of mine, named Hans Georg von Thüngen, who later became a good and honorable man. I sent him to serve a knight under Herzog Ulrich of Württemberg. Others of his young servants dragged my relative to Aichelsdorf, to the residence of Valentin Schott, who was the cause for their traitorous behavior. I learned of this and also learned that he said to let in all other servants of his relative Konrad, if they brought another relative of Götz von Berlichingen. I had many other relatives in the region who were dear to me, wished good things for me and always served me when needed. I knew that Valentin Schott planned to ride to Haßfurt against my relative Ehrhard Truchseß, for whom he waited at this time.

With me was a very smart and experienced servant who became a Pfalzgrafian servant through me. Many other nobles from the region were also accompanying me, numbering an additional sixteen riders with two young squires among them. We now waited for them until they arrived like we predicted, with ten to twelve horses. Because we outnumbered them, we split into two groups. I gave Georg Gebsattel the best horses with the order to cross the river near a windmill. If they did not follow my instruction, they would not able to cross it at all and therefore would not be able to get close enough to the enemy. If they clashed with the enemy first, my group would aid them, and if we met the enemy first than they would do the same for us. In short: I hid in a village behind a barn and planned to let Valentin Schott, Ehrhard Truchseß, and their companions march past me. Then I would follow them closely, like I discussed, with my men, but they detected me before this plan could begin. They retreated up a slope and had their crossbows loaded and lances ready. All of them were wearing heavy armor too. I still moved closer towards them with every step, for no

other reason besides the knowledge that Georg Gebsattel and
his men would come to my aid soon. I became increasingly
terrified the closer I got to the enemy, because I could see more
men the closer I got. It must have been at least twenty-four to
twenty-five riders. Honest to God, I would have probably made
an escape, but I knew that if I did this then the men who I sent
out would all get captured and killed. Therefore, if I did not
follow my own orders, I could have caused great harm to all of
us. They kept their position on top of the hill; I was below them,
and because I did not advance, they had to come down to us.
Erhard Truchseß charged down against a young servant of
mine named Leonhard Schmiedlein. He hung motionless on his
horse afterwards. He was the only Pfalzgrafian servant with
me at the time. Right after this I thrust Truchseß off his horse
so that he fell into dirt along with his coat of arms. This was
our fortune. A companion of his was around us during this, who
shot at me and then threw his crossbow, but both of these
attempts missed me. Because I was fighting with other
enemies at this time, I could not even pay attention to his
attempts at me. Three or four times I had to charge against the
enemy with my ten riders and two squires before the six others
came to our aid. We captured every enemy besides the ones
who escaped right at the beginning. If they all would have
fought as bravely as Ehrhard Truchseß and the one knight of
his who had served under Bernhard von Hutten before this,
then this fight would have turned out badly for us. Every time
I defeated one servant and wanted to go fight another, he
appeared again and demanded my attention. He even knew to
raise my arm and attack below my armor so as to cause a flesh
wound. I was so busy and surrounded that I could not focus on
him enough to defend myself against him alone. The same man
later offered his services to me and said if I accepted him, he
would not ask for any payment for a year. I did not know what
he liked so much about me or my men, but I told him that if he
wanted to join us, he would be treated like any other knight,
even though he gave me such a hard time just a bit earlier in

battle. I did not even need his service at the time, but I was still ready to take such a brave fighter along with us simply because I liked him. I let most of the captured men go on the grounds of some old Urfehde, but I kept Valentin Schott because his kinsman Konrad Schott's servant acted very dishonorably against my relative Hans von Thüngen and my dear Pfalzgraf. In the charge of others, like my squire Georg von Böttigheim and my relative Hans Georg von Thüngen, I kept him under arrest myself. All this happened in a timespan of around two months.

When we released the other prisoners and rode on, we met a cohort of around thirty riders around a quarter mile from where we left. They had tried to follow the other cohort to the grand festival in Haßfurt. This was when I thought that my brother-in-law Sigmund Truchseß, who had married my sister, was among them, and asked him to come out. He asked me who all these riders were, and I told him of all the things that had happened, and he still let me pass. But when they learned it was me who caused all their trouble, they began to say nasty things about me. Now, I still owed Konrad Schott two thousand gulden, which I repaid on St. Peter's Day[126] near Hornberg House in Schweinfurt. I paid him, as agreed, through his wife. When she gave me the receipt and I walked back to my quarters across the market, I met the Markgraf's stable master, who knew me well. He spoke to me in the friendliest way, and warned me that on his way here he had seen around sixty riders. He told me to be careful, because supposedly they were after me. I thanked him greatly and was happy because now I could keep this in mind.

Now I knew without question that Konrad Schott would plan an ambush against me out of revenge. I therefore acted like nothing had happened, went to my quarters, and ate dinner at night around one or two o'clock when all gates were closed. I was afraid they were waiting at all of the gates, but

---

[126] June 29th

especially on the main gate or on the one towards Schweinfurt which I wanted to take, and that's exactly what they did. I therefore decided to take the gate towards Schleichteich. This was not a common path for me and I only took it because I did not have many knights or servants with me. I told them that as soon as we left the gates, they must keep their lances ready. If the enemy appeared before us, we would fight our way through them. But I had chosen the right gate and they did not expect us. The other two gates, like I predicted, were heavily guarded by them. Now I had to make it across the Main to Heidelberg without harm. Before I left, I had sent out a notification to the Kurfürst about what I accomplished and what I planned from there. Near Zellingen I crossed the Main and made it through the territory of Wertheim back to Heidelberg.

CHAPTER TWO:
THE PEASANT WAR

♦

PART I

It is very well known that around this region a huge peasant revolt occurred, which was like no revolt ever seen before.[127] I wrote to my brother Hans von Berlichingen that I wanted to come to him and aid him, because many of the peasants were revolting in Schöntal and I did not want them to harm him. I did this as any honorable brother should, and argued long with the peasant leaders so that they would leave him be. After this the Kaiser sent me into the Weinsberger Valley, and I rode there as first an honorable neighbor but also to tell the prince of my worries and to inform him of what I saw. I spoke to the prince and his captains near Horneck, and told them how the peasants had no cannons or other guns and therefore could not breach the walls. This I did so that the Horneckers could prepare better, because many people were sheltering in the city

---

[127] The many peasant revolts of this time had their roots in a curtailment of many of the traditional rights of the free peasantry. This, combined with the expansion of old taxes and the addition of new ones, created significant tensions, which merged with the general religious disagreements between the masses and the rulers. Already before Luther's teachings, many smaller revolts had occurred, one of which was led by the famous dissident preacher Thomas Münzer. A full-scale peasant war erupted 1524 in Württemberg, which is the revolt described here by Götz.

and they could at least garrison the walls. How the peasants behaved in Weinsberg is known to everyone in the region.[128] From there they marched towards Horneck and captured it without a single sword being swung. I truly wanted to be on the side of the Pfalzgraf in this conflict even though I was not in his service anymore. I wrote Wilhelm von Habern that he should instruct us on how to act, because the peasants were very close and I was afraid they would do the same things to me. I was worried for my children and my pregnant wife. My brother and multiple good friends told me to meet them in a forest near Boxberg, which was named Haßpach. The route there was dangerous, but I still was able to meet up with them even though the devil was causing trouble everywhere. We discussed with which ruler we should align ourselves. I said that I was not aware of any ruler who was in the region besides my own dear master, the Pfalzgraf, who was already trying to aid us. The majority of us therefore agreed to ride to the Pfalzgraf. I had to tell them that I awaited a letter, the contents of which I would tell them as soon as the chance offered itself. As I rode back home, I had to avoid many dangers, and when I arrived, I threw off my armor and asked my wife if any letter had arrived from Heidelberg. She said no. I was shocked because I truly did not know what to do anymore. It was also said that the Pfalzgraf was going to agree to a settlement with the peasants. This left me speechless. My wife supposedly did receive the letter. Upon her reading it out loud to my sister-in-law, she told my wife to not to say a word to me or else we all would be doomed and die. This is why I never received the letter, and all my harm and misfortune arose from that. After I learned of all of this, my sister-in-law was never allowed in my house again, and she indeed never entered my house again.

---

[128] The Weinsberger Bloodbath was the infamous murder of Graf Ludwig of Helfenstein and his companions outside the gates of the city. The Graf and his companions were humiliated and were forced to dance before being forced to run a gauntlet of spears. His wife and son were forced to watch, but spared in the end, and sent to Heilbronn on a wagon of feces.

When the peasants were besieging Grundelsheim, many Berlichingens were there too. Among them was Beringen von Berlichingen, a very old man, and my brother Wolf von Berlichingen. Neither had any idea of what was going on and would have all agreed to a peace settlement. I myself would have not accepted any of this with the peasants and instead always dodged them and rode back home, still hoping for the letter of Heidelberg from Wilhelm von Habern. As long as God remains in Heaven, and I swear on my soul and happiness, till this day, I do not know a single word of this letter. When I arrived home the peasants had already lifted their siege on Grundelsheim and moved on. Their captains sent a messenger to me named Schulheiß, who asked me to meet with them because they had something to discuss. I did not know how to act and I was also afraid they would attack us, therefore causing harm to my family and my servants. I had no people with me who could put up a valid defense and the peasants had the devil in them; my servants and maids were also not doing well. Because of this, I felt forced to ride to them and waited for them near an inn. I was about to go inside when suddenly Max Strumpf came down the stairs and yelled: "Götz, is that you?" I responded: "Yes, it is. Why am I here and what do their leaders want of me?" He spoke: "You have to become their captain." I yelled out: "God be with me, the devil would have to force me himself, why don't you do it instead?" "They asked me to but I can't. If I could do it, if not for my current troubles, I would." I said the same thing as from the start: "I shall not do it and I will go to their leaders myself and will tell them that I shall not be forced." Max said: "Accept the offer, it's the best chance for the rulers and others of nobility." I remained firm in my convictions and rode to the leaders, where I received a warm welcome from everyone, but they told me to go to the other captains who were camping outside the gate in the field. I was supposed to tell them the same thing I told those men. I rode out and spoke to one cohort after another because they were so close to one another. Everywhere where princes, counts, and lords; kinsmen and servants were present, I was received well, except by the Hohenlohians. They stole my horse and surrounded me with the order to surrender. I was supposed to swear an oath to go to Buchen tomorrow, where their camp was, and not to move away without their knowledge if I did not want my wife, child and other nobles to be hurt. I reluctantly and with sadness agreed because I did not want to be strangled to death like they had done with many other brave noblemen from Weinsberg. I still had hope that everything would end well. With a sad heart I went to their camp, praying rather to lie in a Turkish dungeon or anywhere else in the world, and for God to do whatever He wanted to do with me. I therefore joined the peasant troop. God knew my thoughts about this. They took my horse and I had to get off and join their circle. This was where they gave me the title of captain but I still resisted and rejected this because I felt I could not injure my honor and duty in such a way. I also could not agree with the way they behaved. Their behavior and mine were as far apart as Heaven and Earth and I could not justify this to my honor before God, the Kaiser, electors, counts, lords, the knights, the League, or before all the classes, the entire Reich, or the enemies of the Reich. But their begging made no difference. I would not become their captain and play the part of a tyrant, like they had in Weinsberg. I would rather be beaten to death like a sick dog. They admitted that this happened but said it would never happen again.

Then the council of Mainz, around five or six men, and Max Strumpf came to the field (one of them was called Rücker if I remember right). They told me to accept their captaincy in the name of all the rulers and nobles in the Reich, because I could prevent many injustices thereby. I therefore declared: If the peasants restrain themselves and listen to their officers and their masters in the field, if they deal and receive justice according to custom, if they resist against the upper classes in the rightful manner, then I would attempt it with them for eight days. They offered me a different timeline. In the end we agreed on one month, but on the condition that every single one of them had to write a letter to each principality, or city, village, or wherever they were from, no matter how far or near this was, that they would follow my orders to not destroy or burn a single house that belonged to a nobleman or ruler. I took some of the councilors and captains who seemed competent to me, especially one named Wendel Hippler, a very smart man and writer like one could only find among councilmen. He was once a Hohenlohian chancellor, from what I knew, but the Hohenlohe did not give him much respect or credit. With him I set up the contract stipulating their behavior and the requirement that they had to write all regions and principalities to which they called their home. This contract was discussed and accepted by all cohorts and captains, so I believed that the situation was going rather well. But what happened then? They wanted to march from Ammerbach to Miltenberg, where Graf Georg of Wertheim would meet them to reach a settlement with the revolting masses. I started marching there and suddenly the entire bunch set up positions without my knowledge. The reason for this was that a messenger of the peasants had arrived there and written back: They had set out to fight for their freedom, but now they were being commanded to accept their previous condition and to do even more duties on top of that. This caused a great uproar among all the men, such that they raised their fingers[129] and swore that whoever came up with such a contract would be beaten to death. I swear to God that I did not know what they were planning, and returned to them to find out what they wanted to do. A warrior from Heilbronn who was on the side of the peasants came up to me. I got to know him when some of us, like Philipp Echter, Franz von Sickingen, and many of our good friends had besieged Umstadt, near Darmstadt. This man had good intentions with me and listened to all the

---

[129] This gesture, the *Schwurhand*, typically performed with three fingers raised and the pinky and thumb closed, was (and in certain contexts, remains) a customary German gesture of oath-swearing.

speeches of the peasants who I did not know, of and he spoke to me in these short words: "Nobleman, do not ride to the people!" This made me angry and I swore: "On God I shall!" I could not know for what reason I had to be careful. I thought everything would be the same as it was written in the contract, and everything went well. When I then returned to the peasants, I saw a castle burn which was named Willenberg and which was owned by the bishop, which violated the contract we agreed upon. It therefore happened like we discussed before Buchen, where they said they wanted to keep me longer. Back then I declared publicly that they could keep me around for eight days, but that I would lead them in such a way that they would be as tired of me as I was already tired of them. Sadly, my leadership did not last only eight days. Now they marched towards Würzburg and rested outside in the camp near Hattberg arranging another meeting. They did not want to have any masters or noblemen with them and even gave me a vacation before this date. I was never happier, and did not change my original intentions in these days because I was never a hypocrite. I am still not a hypocrite today. I never just said what the peasants wanted to hear, and never agreed with them when they were wrong. They argued successfully to be let into the city and camped near St. Burchard's Church,[130] around the bridge, and even some inside the actual city because they were so many. After I had stayed in Würzburg for a couple of a days, a pious, friendly and charitable man came to me alone, probably because he saw that I tried to lead things honorably and did not agree blindly with everything that had happened. This man warned me, and without a doubt had good intentions. He told me that I was a good and brave nobleman and that I spoke freely and that I was not a hypocrite. But he felt forced to tell me to stop speaking and behaving like this for my own sake. He also warned me not to tell anyone that he had told me this. The peasants had agreed to cut my head off if I

---

[130] At that time located in the old town below Würzburg castle.

did not change my behavior. The people who decided this were a Siebener[131] and a man from the inner council. I was very grateful for this advice because I could tell it was meant genuinely, and I now started thinking on how I should act. The problem was that I was still under oath to serve them for one more month. I had behaved in such a way that they had sent me away after eight days, but I still remained with them for four more weeks so that nobody would call me an oath-breaker. In the end, those were useless thoughts, because I had no means of escape in Würzburg or the camp anyway. Even if God Himself came down to Earth to help me, the peasants would still not have spoken to him, maybe ten or twelve would have stood around him and listened at best. I was also afraid that if I left, they would punish all the other counts, rulers, masters, knights and servants because I broke my oath. This could have been the cause of misfortune for many more nobles than just myself, but the Almighty God gave the Swabian League good luck and they defeated the peasants in Swabia. I saw how quickly the cat crawled up their backs,[132] and they therefore made haste to Lauda from Würzburg. The first camp they made was near the Tauber, then to Krautheim, to Neustadt, and then into the domains of the Hohenlohe. I marched with them to the Hohenlohian town of Adelsfurt. On the same day that they set up the new camp, the four weeks of service I promised to them ended, and I told myself it was time to take my chances. I do not believe that they even were aware that the time had run out, but I knew it exactly, because I had counted every day. With the blessing of God, I hoped to find a way to inform them of this.

With this description every honest and honorable man may see if I was in the wrong or in the right with my actions during the peasant wars. I would also like to hear from every man, if they picked a side or didn't, how I should have acted in front of

---

[131] Franconian slang for someone holding the occupation of a stone-layer.
[132] Meaning to know when it's time to move.

these tyrannical masses with whom I was forced to sign a contract. If there was a chance to behave differently and better, then I would have done so. I did nothing other than to prevent any further damage to the princes, the lords, the Church, and, in short, to everyone of both higher and lower standing, as well as I could. I risked my life for this in every second I was with them, during which I could never be sure if they would not cut off my head. Nobody can accuse me of even stealing or desiring any valuables, because I tried to prevent any looting as well as I could. I never participated in any war where I prayed more often to God for a quick peace and for my honor not to be destroyed than in this peasant war. Further, it is disputed that the Abbey and Convent of Ammerbach offered gifts in the form of two cups to me and all the captains. I noticed myself that this was fraudulent. The others accepted them, but I did not and left them on the table. Where they went, I do not know, but they never entered my home. Many objects were bought by the peasants because they thought they were plated with gold or silver, when most of it was only brass. Leonhard von Thurn lent me the money for this enterprise, which I have since repaid. I did not make a single penny of profit from any of this. The Abbot of Ammerbach still suspected me because a lot of his silver tableware had gone missing, and he believed that I had stolen it from him. But I know and I swear truly on God that I was horribly misjudged in the matter of this precious tableware. This is the truth of the matter, as many honorable people already know. The silver tableware of the Abbot was later found under his bed. Therefore, it is clear that he stole it himself and tried to hoard it. A priest named Friedrich Wohlfarth has since told me this. He is a very pious, honorable, and honest man, from whom nobody ever heard a single lie, and was the priest to myself and my brother in Jagsthausen and Neustadt for over fifty years. The same man heard it from the monks of the Convent of Schöntal, who heard all this, without a doubt, from the monks of Ammerbach (because monks don't hide anything from each other). I have to mention this to save my own honor and the honor of others who are also innocent in this matter and it therefore cannot be left unspoken.

Part II

Further, I feel forced to describe how I had to ride to Georg Truchseß in Stuttgart, because many people had spoken to him already on my behalf. At the time he was the highest captain in all the domains of Württemberg. While I was staying with him, we discussed multiple topics, including the peasant revolt. It happened that he suddenly asked me to enter into the service of Kaiser Ferdinand. I knew at this point very well where I had to go, and where I could find good opportunities, but I had to keep my wife, my children and my poverty in mind. It would be far easier and more honorable to serve our dearest lord the Kaiser, who was the highest captain in the entire Roman Empire, than anyone else. I therefore sold Sir Georg that I would accept no other master, and would wait for his letter, but that I had to be certain that I could rely on his offer. He promised me it was so. I believed him, and rode almost every week to Stuttgart to see how things were. He received me very amicably every time, so that I thought everything was going fine. But God Himself knows what happened to me. I was unjustly thrown down and captured by the League for my honor and gullibility, like I earlier described. If I had chosen my own path, then I would have enacted revenge on every one of my enemies until I met the end that God had ordained for me.

I had to swear an oath that I would surrender myself to wherever they would send me, but I was never told the place where this was supposed to happen, whether in my house or somewhere else. I was just supposed to wait until they told me to leave. Now, everyone who knows me can see how, if I had believed myself guilty of a crime, I could have hidden somewhere, somewhere nobody could have found me in a lifetime, but I did not think I was guilty of any such crime. I could have hidden or escaped in multiple ways, and if I surrendered myself then it would be only under certain conditions. But, like I said, I truly thought I was an innocent man. I had as evidence for such belief the following: A few days before I was supposed to surrender myself, I arrived in Wertheim and met with my dear lord, Graf Georg of Wertheim. He was my dear master and lord, and I trusted him with my life and with everything I owned. I always knew I could rely on him. On this day Thilmann von Bremen was with us. He was a servant of Nuremberg, their master of horse, and, if I remember correctly, their mayor. We all stayed in the same inn. My dear Graf Georg Truchseß sent a messenger to me very late at night, after we had all eaten dinner. The messenger told me that I was supposed to meet with the Graf for breakfast in the castle tomorrow morning. I followed this order and met him waiting for me, because he was a very punctual man. He received me in a friendly manner and offered me his hand. He then asked me in a friendly tone how I would act, and if I truly had the intent to volunteer and surrender myself in Augsburg. I said yes. He disagreed in what I believe could not have been born of a more genuine or friendly intent. He asked me the same question again. I responded yes, and that even if they would throw me into the tower, I would still do it. They knew that I would defend myself well because, as he already knew, I was wholly innocent in the peasant war. He then spoke and said that, as a friend, he did not want to hide anything from me, and that the League had already given orders to arrest me and throw me into the tower as soon as I left the inn. I believed from his words that they had ordered Thilmann of Bremen to do this service, but I was not sure, because he did not say so directly and I did not want to ask. As I said, Sir Thilmann was lodging in the same inn as me. Everything therefore happened exactly as the Graf warned me, with the only difference being that I was thrown in the bottom of the tower and not the top. I spent two years there, and burned through the wealth for which I had worked so very hard. After this I had to spend another quarter of a year in the Tower of Heilbronn because of the Herzog of Württemberg, burned through even more, and was even forced to forfeit to him some of my money. This made already five and a half years of my life that I wasted in jail. This went on until the Kaiser recalled me for his protection, and took me in for his campaign in Hungary. I was thereafter restricted to my residence for another sixteen long years. I never went beyond my own territories, and followed the restrictions forced on me precisely, as God knows. When I was out hunting once and forgot the agreed upon border, I was worried and thought I had crossed it, but the settlement covered all of my territories and my relatives told me that the grass field I was hunting on also belonged to me. I was very happy that I did not cross the border, even though it was by accident.

From all these circumstances every estate, whether prince, count, baron, knight, servant, or any man of high or low standing, may easily see what my intentions and thoughts were. It is known all around that I risked my life and goods for the wellbeing of princes, rulers, nobles, and commoners alike. I threw myself into dangerous and deadly circumstances voluntarily, for no pay, and suffered great misfortune. I shall speak no more of this, because I have already done so enough, and the topic deserves to be put to rest.

Part III

Two years I spent in Augsburg as a prisoner, and already I have often described how I behaved there. I also described how I was warned by both people of high and low standing, but I felt so innocent and trusted justice so dearly that I surrendered myself honorably to Augsburg. When the council of the League questioned me about the peasant war, I always stated that I could justify myself before the law and before God. I asked for a scribe through whom I could write down how things occurred correctly, and thought this was in their interest as well as my own. They agreed, and sent me a learned man who was born in Augsburg. I wrote down how it all occurred myself. The scribe copied it and handed it over to the League. A long time after this, some councilors of the League visited my jail and presented me with the articles of the League, which were completely contradictory to my report. It pained my heart that nobody wanted to believe my honest writing. I shouted with tears in my eyes in fuming anger: He who accuses me of things I did not do, is doing great harm and injustice against me and is trying to make me into a dishonorable villain. I wanted to set the record straight, as was the right of a good and honorable nobleman, with the help of God. Yes, even more: When I was released from prison, I had to swear an oath to surrender myself to the Bishop of Mainz and Würzburg to stand before the court. I followed this oath. The warrant for this was written by the captain of Augsburg named Wolf von Freiburg, who was truly an honorable man, and who meant me well. He visited me many times in the tower out of pity, like a good and proper nobleman. He argued on my behalf before the council of Mainz, and sent the reports of this to my residence while I was busy justifying my actions in front of the Bishop of Mainz and the League in Augsburg. He hoped it would result in an indemnity of around a thousand gulden, more or less. He gave me the well-intended advice to accept this deal and not to dispute it. He would also attempt to pay off those councilors who were favorable to me with a small sum. I instantly wrote him back, stating that I felt wholly innocent in these matters, and would not pay anything to anyone, because justice was on my side. From these actions, every sane man can see how innocent I was in this matter. The councilors then ordered the five judges to release their verdict. This happened and this verdict is still valid until this day. Back then I did not know who the judges were, but found out later when the verdict was made public. I would have been very embarrassed if I knew who these judges actually were at the time, for a few reasons. Only one man of nobility was among them who I knew. It was the Marshal of Pappenheim (the one who had only one eye), who I thought was an honorable man. I was not very pleased with the others because I had fought feuds and squabbles with their rulers in the past, and even captured and held one of the judges as a hostage for a while. But even back then I noticed that he was a good man, and every time I met him after this, he came up to me and offered me his hand. While I held him as a hostage, I had treated him, as best I could, in the way a nobleman should treat any other honorable man. If he is still alive, he will surely agree with this. The other three judges were abbots and prelates, who spoke no good words for me because we were not of the same faith.[133] I knew from the start that I could not expect much good from the leaders of the faith. But they still conducted themselves well as judges, and did not dishonor themselves. I do not want to talk them down here but rather, at least from my perspective, I wish them the best. With this said, I want to let this matter rest.

---

[133] The first indication that Götz had, by this time, officially joined the Reformation.

Part IV

Finally, I want to retell it all one more time so that everyone can truly understand my innocence from this writing, and how dishonorable and unjust my arrest and misfortune was. This would be even easier for me if the Swabian League had not disbanded.[134] I would have without a doubt achieved a different and better settlement for my descendants and I, as I promised it to my wife to soothe her fears while I was in jail. I would use any and all means to prove my innocence, so that the harsh Urfehde that was handed down against me could be eased, as would befit a good and noble knight. I would have surely accomplished this if the court and League, as I said, did not disband. It now is certain that I was innocent in the matters of the peasant revolt, like the council of Mainz and their rulers and advisors declared, a declaration I wholeheartedly agree with. Noble princes and rulers only benefited from my actions, which is why I deserve gratitude, thanks, and honor, not punishment. For their sake I risked my life and limb every day, as I have already said too many times. I would have expected to receive harsher judgment and punishment for the multiple feuds and wars which I led against the League, all of which ended in fairer peace settlements, than for my part in this revolt.

I think that I have justified myself enough about the peasant revolt, and from this point onward, I give all judgment to the Almighty, eternal, and powerful God.

---

[134] The Swabian League dissolved in 1533, torn apart by religious disputes. Unfortunately for Götz, the consequent abandonment of the centralized Swabian legal system that had convicted him ended any chance he had of redeeming himself before a court.

CHAPTER THREE:
SOME RIDING STORIES OUTSIDE OF THE FEUDS

───◆───

Part I

Right after the matters in Rothenburg, I got into other troubles. Sir Melchior Süzel wrote to me in Jagsthausen, where I had just arrived, and asked me if I could hurry to him in Balbach. He meant well by me and was honest in his request. When I arrived, I found many scoundrels in his residence, who he had hired. They told me what this all was about, and why Sir Melchior Süzel wrote me. The Landgraf of Leuchtenberg had arrested a servant of his near Waidwerk, claiming that the hunting rights of that area belonged to him. Süzel desired revenge for this and planned an ambush, because he knew where the Landgraf had planned a future hunt. That's when I said, as the youngest among them, "what will all of you do when the spy who betrayed the Landgraf betrays us, like he did to him?" It happened exactly like I predicted. We left Balbach in the early morning. I gave one servant two young men. One of them was mine, and the other was a servant of Götz von Thüngen. We ordered them to keep their eyes wide open and to scout all the woods and thickets well so that we would not find ourselves ambushed or worse. He and the boys did not find any riders. I left Götz von Thüngen with our horses and went up the valley to the boys, to see if I could spot the enemy. This would give us enough time to give Götz von Thüngen's cohort a chance to escape, if there were any enemy riders. Somehow both the servants and the boys had not seen the enemy. Now Hans von Wald, who originally was from Allsheim, had ridden up ahead of me, and one of the enemies charged at him with a lance. Hans fell off his horse as soon as the enemy came close to him. Another foe rode towards me, but I was not too worried about him because I was well equipped and almost at the forest. He nearly smashed me off my horse, but I held on. As soon as I was safe on my horse again, a third enemy came and thrust me off my horse, because I had not noticed his advance. I instantly got back on my feet and grabbed my spear so that he could not charge at me again. He lost his spear in his first charge, so he drew his sword, and I fended off his attack. During this, Sir Georg Truchseß rode by with the knights of the Landgraf. I was near the forest and was ready to escape into the woods, but another enemy came at me before I could get close enough. He had his lance ready and knocked me off my feet, repeating the manner in which the other had knocked me off my horse. Luckily Sir Georg Truchseß with his knights was already by my side at this point and spoke, "Brother-in-law Götz, is that you?" "Yes," I responded. "Then you will be a prisoner of myself and of the Landgraf." Therefore, I had to go to Balbach as a prisoner. Georg Truchseß only said that I would be his and the Landgraf's prisoner, but did not tell me where I had to surrender myself, how I had to behave, or if I should wait for a letter or a contract. When I arrived in Balbach I saw Hans von Wald, also as a prisoner, like myself with no orders or contract. That's when I said to him: We are young men and we will soon be in chains anyways, so let us go to Castle Lauda ourselves like honorable men. We will send a messenger to Georg Truchseß and tell him that we were young men who were captured by him, but got no orders about where to surrender or what to do, and wished to to ask for them like good and honorable noblemen so that people would not speak badly of us. Because we had no quarrel with him or the Landgraf, we asked him in the friendliest manner to either let us walk free or to give us orders on how to proceed. He then ordered us to go to Boxberg, where we could meet, and where he would instruct us. He came and did not discuss much of anything with us, simply informing us that we would be free men and did not need to swear any Urfehde. Even after this he always treated us in a friendly manner and offered us his services when needed, as if we were old friends. Since then, he remained always my good friend and master, and still is today. Because I once told this story, I did not want to leave it untold here, even though it involved me being thrust off my horse and captured.

Part II

After this, my brother-in-law Franz von Sickingen wrote me requesting that I visit him in the Ebernburg. I followed his demands and made my way from Möckmühl to Heidelberg. Back then I was very sick and felt quite poorly. I felt so sickly that I left my armor, my shirt, and even my arm back in Heidelberg. On the morning of All Saints' Day,[135] I got up very early and did not eat or drink because it was my habit to not eat or drink on holy days until the sun had set. I then marched along the Rhine towards Pfedersheim and had to take a detour from the gate down a steep path, where I could not be seen from the road. I took this path to Alzey without scouting for enemies because I was in such pain that I would have rather cried than fought. When I went away from this path, I found even land, a wine garden, and a seeded field that had been neglected since the harvest. With me was a boy and a servant named Kitz, who noticed the enemy and yelled over: "Master, people are following us!" I responded that we would keep going, hoping to get an advantageous point so that they wouldn't ambush us. I myself thought they were some Pfalzgrafian retainers. When we found a good spot, two of them charged at us like they wanted to devour us, but we had no fear. We were only worried that more would show up along the road. We kept our attention on the path in case more showed up. This was not the case, and we fought with the ones who were already upon us. We challenged them to state who they were, and they did so. When we had fought to a standstill, I asked Kitz who they were aligned with, because I had forgotten. He had forgotten as well. I said that we should make sure who it was we fought, and quickly captured the older man, while Kitz captured the

---

[135] November 1st

younger one, who was the older man's son. As the old man attempted to flee, I seized his crossbow from him, and made him admit who he was. He identified himself as Rudolph von Schwalbach. I then chased him off, away towards the path down which we had come, and Kitz scared his son away into the vineyards. The young Schwalbach turned and shot Kitz' horse through one ear, and Kitz through his buttocks. If my spear had not previously broken, then the old Schwalbach would not have had a good time. My spear-arm was strong, which would have given me a big advantage over to him if the fight had continued. In the end I had to resort to my sword, and with the help of God came off the better. I then shouted for young Kitz to halt. We would hold this position for a while longer in case they come back for one last round. We remained there for around half an hour, but they did not show. While we were fighting around the area, the peasants in the vineyards had bunched up to spectate the fight and kept shouting "Juch, juch, he jenne, he jenne, geth enndt, geth enndt!"[136]

I took the crossbow and brought it with me to Ebernburg. There I told my brother-in-law Franz about what happened to me with Schwalbach, and that I had his crossbow. That's when he said: "With him? He is my servant, and I will settle this trouble." I gave him the crossbow and said that I did not have any ill will towards him, and that he could have his crossbow back. Since then, I never saw him again. On God, I was not there to stir up trouble, because I was sick and had other business to attend to.

---

[136] Basically, commenting on the fight, loosely translating to something like "yeah, yeah, that's it, good block!"

Part III

His Imperial Majesty then freed me from house arrest to aid him in his campaign, on the demand of princes, rulers, and many lords and friends. I spent, like I mentioned earlier, many years in my residence, and he even praised me in his letter for how honorably I followed the rules forced on me by the Urfehde for sixteen years. His captains told me to organize one hundred horses before the Kaiser began his march in fourteen days. I was afraid that I could not fulfill his request, because I was living under arrest and had neither servants nor horses. I wrote them that I could not give a precise number on how many horses I could bring, but that I would do my absolute best and show up with as many as I could gather. I still was able to gather one hundred horses in this short time and lead them to where I was ordered. Also, many of my friends received the same letter, and they joined me on my journey voluntarily, which I thought was very loyal and honorable of them. However, the main army had already been defeated near Pest when we arrived in Austria, and many who fought in that battle fled the region. They crossed paths with us in Bavaria. Nonetheless, we marched on and made camp in a place near Vienna. We remained there for one or two months, but I do not know the specific time when the onset of winter released from our service.

The worst misfortune that ever happened to me and my men was that a bad plague caught us. Death also spread among my people at home, and many noblemen and servants fell victim to it. These are all the adventures I ever experienced during the war. After this I marched back with my men through Bohemia and Neumark, and everyone went back home.

PART IV

In the year 1544, after the Reichstag at Speyer, Kaiser Karl the Fifth[137] marched against France with a large army, which I was part of. We besieged St. Dizier for one or two months, but the city held on even though we bombarded it day and night, and even attempted to storm them when we thought they were short on food and gunpowder. The inhabitants defended themselves bravely, until they agreed to an honorable surrender where it was agreed they would keep their property and honor intact. After this we marched deeper into France and burned everything that was in our path. Then winter came. I agreed with the Kaiser's scorched-earth strategy. I told people before that if he planned to take more cities and land, then he should expect the garrisons to defend themselves just as strongly as we had already witnessed. During this time winter arrived and we remained in place. It would have been very expensive, difficult, and cost a lot of manpower to continue, and we sadly had to leave. At this time, I asked something of a certain warrior, who seemed strong and not incapable, if he is still alive. What his name was, I cannot remember. So that people know somewhat who he was, I will give more detail and say that he was in the service of the current Kaiser, and that he was the captain of the archers. He was with me in France, and the Kaiser's son Maximilian was his master. We got to know one another by talking about various topics, and about which cities and places Kaiser Karl

---

[137] Emperor Charles V, also Charles I of Spain and Austria, Charles II of the Netherlands, and lord of many other territories in Italy, the Americas, and elsewhere through his massive dynastic holdings. Charles V is perhaps the best-known of the Habsburg emperors, the preeminent ruler of his day, and led the Imperial forces during the many European conflicts collectively called the Thirty Years War by later historians.

might want to besiege. One person said he might take Paris, and another spoke of a different city. I then spoke about my view on this matter: If the Kaiser wanted to besiege and take more places and cities whose garrisons are strong, the winter would catch up to us and we would have to retreat. Cost, work, and effort would be for nothing, and we would be at a disadvantage, and even worse, would be dishonored. But if I was Kaiser Karl, then I would destroy and burn everything to the ground, so that in one hundred years everyone would still know that Kaiser Karl had been there, and through that, peace could be achieved.

It happened just as I suggested. We marched deeper into the country and burned and destroyed everything in our sight. I do not know who suggested it to the Kaiser; perhaps he was of the same opinion as me. It took only two days for a French delegation to come to our camps. They begged the Kaiser on their knees for peace. It then came to a very advantageous and honorable peace for the Kaiser. In Cambrai the troops were given leave, and I could visit home. I was very sick before St. Dizier and marched, with permission, along the Ruhr, and remained at home for around nine weeks. Because we still were fighting the enemy, I refused to lay down my armor until the peace and victory was declared.[138] Due to my illness I could not march with the main cohort anymore but had to pace myself as best I could. One young man said this: "The old warrior will never leave the path (and I did not), he will always be right behind us."

---

[138] This was the Peace of Crépy in the year of 1544, that ended the war between the Empire and an alliance of France, the Ottoman Empire, and the county of Jüluch-Cleves-Berg. The conflict was, broadly speaking, an extension of the Italian Wars over the Duchy of Milan, and further involved a dispute over part of the Habsburg inheritance of the Burgundian Netherlands.

Part V

I described all these stories in such detail because it has been many years since many good hearted, brave and honorable people (who still wish good fortune and honor to me until this day, and knew parts of what I did in my life, and how many adventures and dangers I endured against my enemies), approached me and asked me to write down my actions. I could not decline their requests, because they hoped that this would do much good for the reputation of my descendants and I. Every man of lower and higher standing who could read it fairly would find joy in it. I do not care about the people who wish nothing good for me, the ones who speak badly of me out of jealousy and hatred, and who attempt to lie about me to better men, even though I do not deserve any of it. I want to have the last word in telling these stories, and want to write about them honestly so that nobody can say that I did not portray them truthfully. The foundation to all these stories is God Himself, who will be my witness on Judgment Day that I kept all my promises, both as a young man and as an old knight, to both friends and enemy, no matter how important, great, or insignificant they were. I did not break any oath or seal during my punishment, whether during my imprisonment or in some other matter, like a man of true nobility, no matter if before friend or foe. I will be proud about my honesty before God. I did this even though I was warned many times by people of both low and high standing to not volunteer or surrender myself. I remained true to my duties and orders, even for enemies, of which I had many, whether in the Swabian League, or among rulers, and many others besides. Against them I fought both in feud and war, but thanks to God, all of these were justified and settled. I always surrendered myself into their jails when duty and honor demanded, even though I had no security besides my belief in justice. Only a devil would have done otherwise. Even the most distinguished people of the Swabian League said how honorably I acted, even towards enemies who I had caused many grievances against, and who truly hated me. This happened exactly as the good Graf Georg of Wertheim warned me. All this is the truth. The testimony I have given on God's truth, I shall never recant. I shall die with my words, so that at least the Almighty God will show me grace at the end, when I will pass away from this world. If any man says that things happened differently than I have described them in my living testament, then he would do great violence and harm to me.

Part VI

In the end, I shall not deny that the Almighty God gave me victory and luck against all my enemies from my youth onward. All the misfortune I had to endure for so long only came from me trusting my enemies too much in our agreements. Yes should mean yes, and no should mean no. One should follow the agreements one makes with another person. I always believed this, built all my relationships upon this, and hoped others would act the same, and on God would always act the same. It was through being too trusting that I got into all of my misfortunes. But when I did not trust my enemies, which happened many times, then through God's grace and help, it always went well for me and I can say nothing more than to thank God! Through this I learned well how to behave towards my enemies. God the Almighty, forgive me for this!

I count myself rich for all of my dear, brave, and beloved friends. To any man, warriors or not, of high or low standing, emperors, electors, princes, counts, barons, knights, servants, burghers, or others, be they worldly or spiritual, who might find themselves in war or feud, I do not wish to hide any of this from them and their good hearts, as a warning and as an example.

Now help us God, in His eternal word,
Our poor bodies here, and our souls there,
Protect us, Almighty God,
From eternal death. Amen.
Götz von Berlichingen, to Hornberg.